Cyril is a retired London Firefighter, who at now works for Transport for London, advising on aspects of safety. He is married to Jackie and together they have three grownup children, Georgina, Anne-Marie and Spencer. At the time of writing they have one grandson, Coray, from his daughter Georgina and partner Ahmet.

Cyril has a passion for trivia and entertaining, and loves socialising. In his past, Cyril used to manage public houses prior to his service in the London Fire Brigade, and this book is a combination of his life and passions.

Dedication

To my wife, Jackie, and family, who have suffered whilst smiling, during the writing of and research for this book.

Cyril O'Brien

A History Of London Through Beer Goggles

AUSTIN MACAULEY PUBLISHERS™

LONDON · CAMBRIDGE · NEW YORK · SHARJAH

A CIP catalogue record for this title is available from the British Library.

ISBN 9781788234887 (Paperback)
ISBN 9781788234894 (Hardback)
ISBN 9781788234900 (E-Book)
www.austinmacauley.com

First Published (2018)
Austin Macauley Publishers Ltd™
25 Canada Square
Canary Wharf
London
E14 5LQ

Acknowledgements

I would like to acknowledge my old boss in the London Fire Brigade, Dave Pike, who since retiring has written and published various books, and without his help and support I would still be going around in circles. Thanks.

Table of Contents

London's History through Beer Goggles!
Introduction

Having long been an advocate of trivia, and the gathering of perceived useless information, I came to the conclusion that whilst I had some time on my hands, why not put some of the accrued knowledge down on paper. I know there are lots of reference books out there, and with the internet you can find out most things if you have a mind to. However, sometimes it's nice to get out and see history in the flesh. So how could I present something that would be fun, informative yet different?

Well my other passions include; drinking and socialising (not necessarily in that order, or maybe it is!), so I had this idea why not combine the two, and link them to the greatest city in the world, hence the idea of seeing London through beer goggles.

This book will take you on a journey across London, looking at some little-known facts as well as the more established ones, and to make it interesting I have planned some stop-offs along to way, namely Pubs. I must stress at this point it is not an essential part of this experience to consume alcohol at each establishment as soft drinks are available, but if you are drinking, please remember to stay safe whilst crossing roads etc., and do not forget to eat something.

So in essence this book is series of pub crawls, with history entwined within the journey. I have tried to keep the travel distances achievable within crawl, although the more enthusiastic participant may wish to combine one or more crawls, and I have set out the book to facilitate this by starting the next crawl start point near to the end of the previous one.

A note on authenticity, scholars may debate what is actual historical fact, and what is legend or folklore. I am not a historian! Where I can I have included my research bibliography at the end of the book, but some facts are passed down through word of mouth and hence become folklore or legend, (one definition of folklore is; "the traditional beliefs, customs, and stories of a community, passed through the generations by word of mouth" (Google)). But that does not mean we should ignore them. Also, it is hard to prove or disprove the presence of ghosts. So rather than refer to this as an historical reference book, see this as collection of facts, folklore and legends put into a framework whereby you will know more useless information as a consequence of these 'crawls' providing you do not get too drunk! **Happy Crawling!**

Crawl 1
East of the City to London Bridge
(Smugglers to Rowers)

This part of the city was the lifeline when the city formed, docks provided all type of goods from the River. However, there was also Justice, prisons and a few pubs! As you walk around this part of the city its history envelops you. Apart from the Romans and all the stuff they left! We still have churches which date back to 675 AD. Living in a city we sometimes take our history from granted …. not today!

Remember the immortal words of Old Blue Eyes (Frank Sinatra)

"Alcohol may be man's worst enemy, but the bible says love your enemy."

Pubs on Route: (Approximately 2.7 miles)

Prospect of Whitby – Turners Old Star – The Captain Kidd – Town of Ramsgate – The Dickens Inn – Hung, Drawn and Quartered – Monument

Starting Point:

Prospect of Whitby Public House:

Address: 57 Wapping Wall, London E1W 3SH
Phone: 020 7481 1095
Nearest Overground: Wapping
Hours:

Saturday	12pm–12am
Sunday	12–10:30pm
Monday	12–11pm
Tuesday	12–11pm
Wednesday	12–11pm
Thursday	12–11pm
Friday	12pm–12am

- The Oldest Riverside Pub!" as you will see later in this book, this title is disputed, but suffice to say it is definitely one of the oldest riverside pubs. So a good place to start our first crawl.

- A traditional British Pub which can be dated back to the 1520s. The floor is the original flagstone floor, and it has a pewter topped bar, which is rarely seen nowadays, and within the structure are some barrels and parts of ships masts.
- From here you can gain spectacular views of River Thames, and it's because of this location its initial clientele was people who worked on the river, or those who had some nefarious business deals needed the river, namely pirates and smugglers!
- Famous customers included Samuel Pepys and Judge Jeffreys (The Hanging Judge), it is common folklore that the Judge would sentence the criminal and come along and watch them hang whilst have his lunch. Indeed, there is a commemorative gallows at the rear of the pub showing where the site of *Execution Dock, may have been, although the precise location is once again disputed.
- The pub also has had some film/television credits to its name, for example, in the 1956 film: D–Day the sixth of June Robert Taylor and Dana Wynter's characters are seen having a drink, and the pub also briefly appeared in an episode of Only Fools and Horses.

Ghost Alert

If you have a penchant for the darker side of life/or after life, The Prospect of Whitby is believed to one of London's Haunted Pubs with Judge Jeffreys returning to check up on his 'good deeds!'

Nowadays the customers tend to be more law abiding, and the pub has a nice atmosphere.

Execution Dock

- To understand why London had an Execution Dock we have to look back to the times when the Port of London was the biggest port in the world. The River Thames flowing through London directly out to sea made it an important trading port which it has maintained for centuries. Wapping due to its location became the last point at which the Admiralty held jurisdiction. One of its responsibilities was to punish any crimes committed at Sea, and the accused were put on trial and if found guilty executed in London.

- Now at the time, London's prisons had their own Gallows and Hangmen, however the Admiralty in their wisdom wanted to ensure that any execution was a very public affair and used as a deterrent to others thinking of straying from the path of the law.

- Hanging people on the waterfront, meant that all river vessels would be able to see the poor unfortunate hanging from the gallows.

- The Admiralty presided over many crimes and criminals, and not just British 'jack tars', indeed they were happy to bring to justice anyone engaging in a 'sea based crime.' Some crimes such as 'piracy' carried an automatic death by hanging if found guilty, with the additional bonus of it having to be carried out in a public place.

- Now one would think that by issuing a death sentence would mean that from that point onwards a standard process would follow, no! Even in death, life is not fair or equal. The way we have executed people across the centuries has varied depending upon one's class, and the crime committed.

- Indeed, in times gone by beheading was deemed a more preferential way to die, rather than burning at the stake, or hanging etc., and even that was divided into whether or not they used an axe or sword. We will cover this more later on in this crawl but for now let's deal with the hangings at Execution point.
- How could they make any sort of distinction between being hanged! Well if you were a pirate you were hung with a shorter rope as an extra punishment. By the rope being shorter meant it was unlikely that you would break your neck, but hang there until you were strangled to death. The bodies movements i.e. legs flailing soon attracted the term The Marshalls Dance, as it was the High Court Marshall who oversaw these executions.
- The other difference here at Execution dock was that the body had to remain in situ until three tides had ebbed and flowed over them. However, if you done something really heinous your body was then tarred and placed along the River Thames as a reminder of what would happen to you should you wish to take up piracy and got caught.
- But things were not all bad! Whilst being paraded along the streets from the Prison at London Bridge, past the Tower of London to their execution the condemned they were allowed to stop off at the Turks Head tavern (which is now a café, and we will pass on this crawl) on the way and have their last quart of ale. The procession was led by the Deputy Marshall carrying a silver oar to denote the authority of the admiralty.
- One famous or infamous character which was hanged at Execution dock was Captain Kidd who was sentenced for Piracy and Murder in 1701. Legend has

it that at the first attempt the rope broke, and he had to go through the whole process again. Once dead his body was hung on a gibbet at Tilbury Docks for three years in an attempt to deter others who thought piracy was positive move in the employment market!

- The last executions took place here on 16th December 1830, Messrs George Davis and William Watts, both sent to heaven or hell for piracy.

On Wards and Upwards:

Route: Upon leaving the Prospect of Whitby turn left along Wapping Wall until you reach the corner of Wapping Lane. Turn up Wapping Lane and proceed along there until you come across St Peter's Church London Docks.

- This has been awarded a Grade 1 Listing, and is one of only 13 such buildings in Tower Hamlets. Begun in 1865, it had to be restored after WWII bomb damage (as Wapping was on the direct route followed the Nazi bombers as they made their way along the Thames towards London, and would dump a lot of their bombs over this area). As with most things you should never judge the book by its cover as the dull exterior hides a splendid interior and some lovely stained-glass windows, worth a quick look!

Route: Moving back into Wapping Lane turn left, then take the first right into Watts Street. Carry on down this street until you reach Turners Old Star Public House on the right, our next stop.

Turners Old Star Public House

Address: 14 Watts St,
London E1W 2QG
Phone: 020 7481 1879
Nearest Overground: Wapping
Hours:

Saturday	12pm–1am
Sunday	12–10:30pm
Monday	12–11:30pm
Tuesday	12–11:30pm
Wednesday	12–11:30pm
Thursday	12–11:30pm
Friday	12pm–1am

- **Joseph Turner (1775 – 1851)**

  Turner was born in Maiden Lane, Covent Garden, London, England. His father, William Gay Turner (27 January 1738 – 7 August 1829), was a barber and wig maker. His mother, Mary Marshall, became increasingly mentally unstable, perhaps, in part, due to the early death of Turner's younger sister, Helen Turner, in 1786. She died in 1804, after having been committed to a mental asylum in 1799.

- **From the plaque outside the pub**

  Brought up in London, Turner was always fascinated by the Thames. Water and ships were a major source of inspiration in his work and the riverside area of London was to remain his home base all his life. Turner was held in high regards by his contemporaries, and was rewarded with both critical acclaim and considerable wealth. Although something of a 'society' figure, he was more at home among the bustle and debris of London's Docklands.

- **Turners Secret Life**

  Turner was exceptionally secretive, especially over women. From the age of twenty-five he was to keep several mistresses, who were to bear him four illegitimate children. Although he never married, women always played an important part of Turners life. His vigorously sensual side was to emerge in the copious quantities of erotic drawings discovered amongst the Turner bequests upon his death. These were supposedly executed during the weekends of drunken debauchery amid the Dockside taverns of Wapping.

- **'Puggy Booth'**

  In 1833 Turner met Sophia Booth, a widowed landlady from Margate who was to become his mistress until his death in 1851. When Turner inherited two cottages in the dockland area of Wapping, he converted them into a tavern and installed Mrs Booth as proprietor. He named the tavern 'The Old Star'. To maintain his secrecy during their life together Turner adopted her surname. This, combined with his five-foot height and portly physique was to earn him the nickname 'Puggy Booth'.

Route: After a quick libation its back on the road, turn right back into Watts street and follow straight on to Tench Street, follow this around all the way until you come across the Turks Head Café on the left. Carry on down Tench Street and straight across to Scandrett Street where you come across ST Johns Old School on the left. Staying on Scandrett Street all the way until come across a T-junction. Now turn left and head down Wapping High Street until you reach the Captain Kidd Pub.

On your route:

The Turks Head

This site was previously a pub, where condemned criminals stopped for the last quarter ale before going to Execution Dock. A record of the history is written on a plaque outside:

- *"This former public house has a special history. During World War II it was run by its eccentric landlady Mog Murphy and stayed open all hours for service personnel seeking news of their loved ones.*

- *After a vigorous campaign in the 1980s led by Maureen Davies and the wild women of Wapping, the Turks Head Company, a charity they set up to improve local life, bought the derelict building from the council and restored it.*
- *The income from the rents of the café and studios above pays for charitable activities"*

St Johns Old School

Although founded in 1695 – a year after the parish of Wapping itself – the building you see now dates 'only' to 1765. These are two of the finest Bluecoat statues in London, with the costume details outstanding. The separate boys and girls entrances are clearly marked.

These distinctive figures mark a charity school, many dating back to the mid-16th century, with the costumes being normal school attire of the period. Blue was used for charity school children because it was the cheapest dye available for clothing. Socks were dyed in saffron as that was thought to stop rats nibbling the pupils' ankles.

The Captain Kidd Public House

Address: 108 Wapping High St, London E1W 2NE
Phone: 020 7480 5759
Nearest Overground: Wapping
Hours:

Saturday	12–11pm
Sunday	12–10:30pm
Monday	12–11pm
Tuesday	12–11pm
Wednesday	12–11pm
Thursday	12–11pm
Friday	12–11pm

- According to the excellent London's Riverside Pubs by Tim Hampson, the Captain Kidd is an old warehouse and was only converted into a pub in the late 1980s. Named after Captain Kidd who was hanged at nearby Execution Dock in 1701 for piracy, the building has no connection with him.
- William Kidd was kept in Newgate Gaol before his hanging, and on Sunday May 18th, 1701, he heard his final sermon from the chaplain, but Kidd still hoped for a reprieve, the others who had been condemned with him for piracy received it – all except one, an Irishman named Darby Mullins.
- On the afternoon of the 23rd May 1701, they were taken, with two Frenchmen who were also to die, from Newgate in two horse-drawn carts, guarded by marshals and led by the Admiralty Marshal and the silver oar which was the Admiralty's symbol. To the chaplain's horror, Kidd seemed the worse for drink (what did he have to lose!) At five o'clock, low tide, they reached Execution Dock at Wapping, a few yards below Wapping Old Stairs, in the presence of a large and lively crowd.
- There was a permanent gallows for pirates there and after the hanging the corpses were customarily chained to a post on the foreshore, where they were left until three tides had flowed over them, as an example. Kidd spoke to the crowd, warning all ship-masters to learn from his fate.
- Then the four men were hanged, but Kidd's rope snapped and he fell to the ground with the noose around his neck, still alive and dazed (talk about lucky! Phew! Got away with that!).
- But no! The chaplain prayed over him once more and he was hoisted up again, and that was that. His body

was taken to be hanged in chains at Tilbury Point. Kidd was in his mid-fifties when he died.

- The line between piracy and government-sponsored privateering was narrow and he does not seem to have been the typical swashbuckling pirate of popular fiction. He did not maroon anyone or make people walk the plank, but legends clustered around him which turned him into a name to conjure with.

Route*:* Now travel back down Wapping High Street passing the Met Police river station on the left. Continue on this road until you reach the Town of Ramsgate Pub on your right-hand side.

Metropolitan Marine Policing

- The MPU enjoys a rich history dating back to its formation in 1798 when magistrate Patrick Colquhoun and Master Mariner John Harriott set up the Marine Policing Establishment to combat an epidemic of theft that blighted the cargo ships and their precious cargos that entered and left the Pool of London.
- The initial set up costs to provide 30 officers and sufficient boats amounted to £4200. It is estimated that after its first year of operation, it had recovered £122,000 worth of cargo and saved countless lives. The ill feeling amongst the thieves that the Marine Police were denying them of their livelihood was such that it sparked a riot outside the Wapping Police Office.

Wapping Coal Riot:

"On 2nd July 1798, officers of the West India Merchants and Planters Marine Police Institute, generally considered to be this country's earliest organised police force, first patrolled the crowded waters of the River Thames from their headquarters at Wapping New Stairs. By October 16th of that same year, they had lost their first man killed on duty when Gabriel Franks (Master Lumper) attained the dubious privilege of being the first ever police officer to be killed in the execution of his duty. The following paragraphs are a synopsis of the facts relating to the incident as recorded in the official trial transcript from the archives of the Old Bailey.

- Perhaps the first thing to note is that the embryonic Thames River Police as founded by John Harriott and Patrick Colquhoun, was organised rather differently from the manner in which we might envisage a modern police force being run. The job titles within the force were certainly very different from those of today. The men who made up the river police were described as watermen, surveyors and lumpers.

- There were only a very few constables in the force (five initially) and they were mostly employed on land patrols. Harriott recognised that a considerable amount of crime was committed by those people employed in unloading vessels arriving in the Port of London. He reasoned that if you could guarantee the honesty and integrity of those men employed in 'lumping' cargoes off the ships, then you would indeed go a long way to cutting down the thefts that occurred from those vessels.

- Thus, the lumpers employed in unloading vessels under the protection of the Marine Police Office were those with a reputation for honesty and they were accordingly paid above the usual rate because of that.

- These men were actually seen to be as much a part of the Marine Police Office as, say the watermen, surveyors or even the magistrates themselves. That becomes an important factor in the story that follows.

- Coal was an important commodity in London at that time and its theft was perceived to be a major problem by the Thames Magistrates. Harriott and Colquhoun were both determined to stop the 'coal markets', which were openly held in the streets of Wapping.

- At these markets, coal unlawfully appropriated by coal heavers during the course of their work was on open sale. Unsurprisingly, the coal heavers took a dim view of any such attempt at cutting their extra income, which they saw as an unofficial 'perk' of the job.

- On the evening of 16th October 1798 three persons were standing trial at the Thames Magistrates Court attached to the Marine Police Office. They were two coal heavers and one watchman's boy. All three were accused of theft of coal. They were all convicted and each fined forty shillings. As they left the building, friends arrived at the court and paid the fines.

- Upon leaving, one of the three, Charles Eyers was met by his brother, James, who said *"Damn your long eyes, have you paid the money?"* Charles said *"Yes, I have."* James then took his brother by the collar, dragged him toward the door and said *"Come along and we shall have the money back or else we shall have the house down!"* Within a very short period of time a hostile crowd had gathered outside the police office and stones and rocks were being directed against the windows. The action that was to follow was to leave two men dead and another wounded.

Death in the High Street.

- From the transcript of the trial we can see that from the beginning of the disturbance events moved swiftly. Those inside the office secured the building as best they could but plainly considered themselves to be in some considerable danger. When a large stone smashed through a window an officer, (Perry) took a pistol and fired a shot into the crowd, that shot killed a rioter (Unnamed). The crowd seemed to quieten and withdraw slightly. Perry implored the magistrates to leave the building where he obviously felt at great risk. Having gone into the street, Colquhoun read the Riot Act to the crowd, ordering them to disperse. They did not.
- Gabriel Franks was a master lumper employed by the Marine Police Office. It would appear that at the time of the riot, Franks was in the nearby Rose and Crown public house in the company of some friends. Upon hearing the commotion, he made his way to the police office with two other men (Peacock and Webb) and asked to be admitted. He was told however that nobody was to be allowed in or out of the building.
- Franks decided to return to the main street and observe the disturbance with the intention (it would seem) of gathering useful information and evidence. Franks instructed Peacock to keep observation on one particularly active rioter whilst he himself went to try and secure a cutlass for their protection.
- Peacock stated that about a minute later he heard a shot ring out from the direction of the Dung Wharf,

he then heard Franks cry out that he had been shot. It appears from the evidence that the two shooting incidents happened in quick succession.

- Indeed, one witness (Elizabeth Forester) tried to persuade the court that both men had been killed by the one shot fired from the police office. Her evidence was easily discredited and several witnesses referred to her as a woman of *"Infamous character"*.

- Franks did not die immediately but lived on for several days, during which time he was conscious and apparently lucid. His injuries were treated by William Blizzard, a surgeon at the London Hospital. During this time Franks was questioned about the incident but he plainly had no idea as to who had fired the shot that, he knew was about to kill him, more than anyone else.

- The identity of the person who pulled the trigger and fired the fatal shot will never be known and we can only speculate as to the motive for the killing. Franks would have been known as someone associated with the police office and may well have been deliberately singled out for revenge as he walked alone to towards the Dung Wharf. Or, he may simply have been in the wrong place at the wrong time and got in the way of a stray bullet.

- James Eyers, the man whose behaviour at the court was the initial spark that ignited the incident, was eventually arrested and charged with the murder of Gabriel Franks. There was never any evidence to suggest that he had actually fired the fatal shot. Indeed, the only witness to place him anywhere near to Franks during the incident was the discredited Elizabeth Forrester.

- The prosecution simply held that because of his actions in starting the riot, he was, in law responsible for Franks' death and demanded that he should face the death penalty... a view that the court obviously shared.
- On the 9th January 1799 James Eyers was convicted of the murder of Gabriel Franks. He was sentenced to be hanged the following Monday morning. In passing sentence the judge, Mr Justice Heath, donned the traditional black cap and spoke the usual and well-known phrase... *"Prisoner – May the Lord have mercy upon your soul."* Eyers replied *"Amen, I hope he will"*
(http://www.thamespolicemuseum.org.uk/h_wapping coalriots_1.html).

As you walk along Wapping High Street look see if you can spot the old cannons being used as bollards outside number 94 opposite Wapping Rose Garden.

- Is this rumour or fact? In all probability it's a bit of both. After the defeat of the French at Trafalgar in 1805, the British used to strip the French ships and reuse anything of value. However, with the cannons they were not the correct size to try and fit onto British ships. Waste not, want not! The Brits decided instead to use them as street furniture throughout the East London.
- As it appeared this was a good idea and well-liked by the public once all the original cannons had been utilised, replicas were made and these started to appear more and more on London streets. They are still being made today, with their unusual shape being an iconic feature of London's streets.
- Most of the original cannon-bollards have been replaced by now however, a few can still be seen.

One is on the South Bank near to Shakespeare's Globe Theatre which is an original French cannon from the Battle of Trafalgar. We will see this on a later crawl. Onwards to our next pub which is just down the road.

The Town of Ramsgate Public House

Address: 62 Wapping High St, London E1W 2PN
Phone: 020 7481 8000
Nearest Overground: Wapping
Hours:

Saturday	12pm–12am
Sunday	12–11pm
Monday	12pm–12am
Tuesday	12pm–12am
Wednesday	12pm–12am
Thursday	12pm–12am
Friday	12pm–12am

- The first pub on the site probably originated during the Wars of the Roses in the 1460s and was called The Hostel. During more peaceful times in 1533 it became known as The Red Cow, a reference to the bar maid working at the time.

- The notorious Judge Jeffreys was caught outside the ale house as he tried to escape disguised as a sailor on a collier bound for Hamburg after the Glorious Revolution of 1688, which overthrew King James ll.
- Presiding over the Bloody Assizes after Monmouth's unsuccessful rebellion against James ll, Judge Jeffreys had taken great pleasure in sending hundreds to their execution, and in abusing their attorney's, which was a costly mistake as one of them recognised him resulting in his capture.
- During the Glorious Revolution, when James II fled the country, Jeffreys stayed in London until the last moment, being the only high legal authority in James's abandoned kingdom to perform political duties.
- When William III's troops approached London, Jeffreys tried to flee and follow the King abroad. He was captured in a public house in Wapping, now named *The Town of Ramsgate*.
- Reputedly he was disguised as a sailor, and was recognised by a surviving judicial victim, who claimed he could never forget Jeffreys' countenance, although his ferocious eyebrows had been shaven. The quondam chancellor was terrified of the public when dragged to the Lord Mayor and then to prison "for his own safety". He begged his captors for protection from the mob, who intended "to show him that same mercy he had ever shown to others".
- He died of kidney disease (probably pyelonephritis) while in custody in the Tower of London on 18 April 1689. He was originally buried in the Chapel Royal of Saint Peter ad Vincula in the Tower.
- In 1766 the pub became known as Ramsgate Old Town and by 1811 it had again taken on a new

identity known as The Town of Ramsgate. The reference to Ramsgate became about after the fishermen of Ramsgate who landed their catches at Wapping Old Stairs.

- They chose to do so as to avoid the river taxes which had been imposed higher up the river close to Billingsgate Fish Market. Ramsgate harbour of 1850 features in the pub sign and is also etched on the mirror near the entrance to the pub.

- As for the Wapping Old Stairs next door, they also have a bloody history. If you visit during low tide, you can still see the post to which condemned pirates were chained to drown as the tide rose. The Stairs were made famous in Rawlinson's cartoon and Dibden's poems. John Banks came here, with Captain Bligh to inspect the Bounty before purchasing it for the ill-fated voyage to Tahiti.

- More happily, many returning sailors were met by their sweethearts on the Old Stairs at the end of a voyage. The silent question that must have been on many sailor's lips is answered by a verse on the wall of the pub.

"Your Polly has never been faithless she swears, since last year we parted on Wapping Old Stairs."

Route: As you come out of the pub stay on Wapping High Street (heading away for the Met Police marine station), as you go straight on you will see the Hermitage Riverside Memorial Gardens. Stay on Wapping High Street until you reach St Katherine's Way. Turn left and follow the road until you reach St Katherine's Dock where you will see the Dickens Inn on your right.

Hermitage Riverside Memorial Gardens

A memorial paid for by solely private money, as a gift to the locals. This is a place where friends and families can come, but also where a new generation of East Enders can learn about the sacrifices of other locals. The people of the East End never once flinched during the blitz, indeed, the Blitz Spirit was born in Wapping among the working class people in the air raid shelters who then cleared away the rubble and went to work in the docks and the factories.

- Artist Wendy Taylor, sculpted the dove memorial as it represents hope, with the cutaway shape of the bird symbolising the civilians lost during the 1939-45 war.

- It is a fitting memorial to the time Britain stood alone, after the Fall of France, when London was being bombed continuously for 57 consecutive days between 1940 and 1941 by the Luftwaffe attempting to demoralise the population and knock Britain out of the war.

- The Port of London was a strategic target. The docks were easy to locate for Hitler's bombers, following the distinctive, winding course of the Thames.

The Dickens Inn

Address: Marble Quay, St
Katharine Docks, St Katharine's
Way, London E1W 1UH
Phone: 020 7488 2208
Nearest Tube: Tower Hill
Hours:

Sunday	12:00 – 22:30
Monday	11:00 -23:00
Tuesday	11:00 – 23:00
Wednesday	11:00 – 23:00
Thursday	11:00 – 00:00
Friday	11:00 – 00:00
Saturday	11:00 – 00:00

- The Dickens Inn is now one of the most famous and most successful pubs on The River Thames loved by locals and tourists alike. Famous visitors to the venue have included Joan Rivers and Katie Melua. With the addition of a large function suite, The Dickens Inn can now cater for parties from 4 to 150 for any occasion imaginable. One critic described The

Dickens Inn as "The most atmospheric spot in the whole of London".

- The original building stood on a Thames side site just east of its current location. In the 1820s its timber frame was encased in a more modern brick shell to make the warehouse conform to the architectural style of St Katharine Docks masterminded by Thomas Telford, the celebrated Scottish civil engineer.

- It could not, however, stay on its original site as this had been earmarked for housing under the St Katharine's dockland development scheme. The 120-tonne timber shell was therefore moved some 70 metres and erected on its present site.

- The original timbers, tailboards and ironwork were used in the restoration and the building reconstructed in the style of a three-storey balconied inn of the 18th century. When Cedric Charles Dickens, grandson of the famous author Charles Dickens, formally opened the Inn in May 1976 he said My Great Grandfather would have loved this inn.

- This is surely true as the writer who can fairly be known as the world's favourite story teller knew Thameside and East London intimately. His works are stocked with characters and scenes memorably linked with the area.

St Katherine's Dock:

A thousand years of dramatic history

- The Docks are built on a site with over 1000 years of dramatic history. The roots of the buildings on today's site can be traced back to the 10th

Century when King Edgar gave 13 acres of land to 13 Knights, with the right to use the land for trade.

- There is evidence of there having been a dock at St Katharine's since 1125 and throughout the ages it has housed a Hospital and Monastery.

- The first use of the name St Katharine Docks has been traced back to Elizabethan times, when the area around the hospital was thriving with busy wharves. By the end of the 18th Century, St Katharine's was a prosperous settlement with its own court, school and alms houses along with the hospital the area housed around 3000 people.

- However, the Industrial Revolution came to London, and the River Thames became a super-highway for the rapidly growing city. London's existing docks could not handle the amount of trade and Parliament authorised the construction of new, purpose built docks."

(http://www.skdocks.co.uk/the-docks/our-heritage)

This is a lovely place to stay and relax whilst watching the world go by, a hidden gem in the heart of London.

Route: As you come out of the Pub head back to St Katherine's Way and follow the road until you reach Tower Bridge Road. Turn onto Tower Bridge Road towards the Tower of London, keep left and follow Tower Hill which morphs into Lower Thames Street, and the next hostelry 'Hung Drawn and Quartered' is on your right.

This is a major historic area, with facts, legends and folklore in abundance.

So where to start, before our next pit stop let's take some time to look around; you may even want to visit the Tower, but rather than go over all of the history of the Building here are some titbits about the place.

- Right, lets walk up Tower Bridge Road itself (be wary of heavy traffic) apart from the fantastic structure of Bridge (you can even walk up to the top if you so wish), what else could be there to see. Well as you walk up to the bridge, lamp posts can be seen on both sides of the road, painted in colour of the bridge, however upon closer inspection one pillar on the side of the road leading back to the Tower, looks slightly different, and has no lamp on it. This is the second pillar after coming under the road arch of the bridge on the north side. This is in fact a chimney!
- This was for the Royal Fusilier's room under the bridge which would have been used by the guards when on duty protecting the Tower of London. The room would have had a coal fire and what we see above on the bridge is the where the smoke would have come out.
- The London Clean Air Act came into force on 1956 and smokeless fuel could only be used in urban areas. This was probably the end of this room.

Ghost Alert

Now is the Bridge Haunted?
- A little-known fact (unless you have done the tour previously) is that beneath the North Tower is Dead Man's Hole, this was the site of a morgue, and although no longer in use, you can still see the river access.
- Apparently, due to the river currents, people who were either murdered, committed suicide or died accidently and ended up in the River due to the currents would end up here.

- If you make your way down to the old morgue, see if you can spot the pike hook on the wall, which may have been used to hook the dead bodies out of the River (if this is true or not depends on who you talk too).
- They were then removed from the river and laid out in the morgue awaiting identification. So some people believe that some of the tormented souls still frequent the place.

Okay back to our route.

Now we come to the Tower of London on the left, I am not going to cover all the history of the Tower as it could take a book on its own, but here are some facts about the Tower and its infamous history.

- First started to be built by William the Conqueror in the around 1070 – 1080s and added to by successive Monarchs.
- First Prisoner was Bishop Ranulf Flambard, chief tax-collector, was imprisoned under King Henry I. He was the Tower of London's first prisoner and also became its first escapee.
- Flambard had made himself unpopular doing King William Rufus's dirty work, collecting large taxes and becoming very rich. When William died, his brother Henry I accused the Bishop of extortion and sent him to the White Tower in chains.
- Flambard used the cover of the feast of Candlemas to make a bold escape. He had a rope smuggled to him in a gallon of wine. He invited his guards to join him for a great banquet. When they were completely drunk and snoring soundly, he seized his chance. He tied the rope to a column which stood in the middle of a window and, holding his Bishop's staff, he climbed down the rope. At the foot of the tower, his

friends had horses ready and he galloped off to safety. (http://www.hrp.org.uk/tower-of-london/history-and-stories/palace-people/ranulf-flambard).

- First animals (lions) arrive at the Tower in 1210. Part of the Tower was used as a menagerie for over 600 years.
- In 1483, King Edward IV sons (the young Princes), sent to the Tower and never seen again.
- In 1605: Guy Fawkes is tortured at the Tower following the failed Gunpowder Plot to assassinate James I and blow up Parliament
- In 1835 Tower Menagerie closes. The animals are transferred to the new London Zoo
- In 1941 the last execution is done at the Tower. Josef Jakobs was killed by firing squad, and is the only person I can find ever who has been executed by firing squad whilst sitting in a chair. He was given the chair to sit on, as he an injured his ankle.
- In fact, The Tower itself was historically reserved for the super-celebs. Only seven executions are recorded on Tower Green, within the complex. These include the termination of three queens: Anne Boleyn, Catherine Howard and Jane Grey. The rest were executed outside the Tower in the now Trinity Square Gardens. (we will see this later)
- The Ravens: Legend has it the six ravens must be at the Tower or the Tower and the Monarchy will fall!
- No one is sure when they first arrived but it is documented that King Charles II upon hearing of the legend ordered that there will always be at least six Ravens at the Tower. One of the Beefeaters is designated as the Raven Master.

- In its 900 year history the Tower has been a Royal Palace, a prison a fortress a place of execution, a menagerie, an arsenal, a mint and a Jewel House.

As we travel along Tower Hill there two things to pick up on. One on the right, is Trinity Square Gardens. Inside the gardens the Execution Memorial is on the approximate spot of where the scaffold stood and has a number of plaques listing the names and year of execution of many of the more well-known victims. The central plaque states that the memorial is:

- *"To commemorate the tragic history and in many cases the martyrdom of those who for the sake of their faith, country or ideals staked their lives and lost.*
- *On this site more than 125 were put to death. The names of some of whom are recorded here."*

At our next watering hole there is more information within the pub about this.

But before we imbibe again it is worthwhile just to detour a little, turn down towards the Tower of London Ticket Office at the end you will see this structure.

This is the entrance to the Tower Subway.

Tower Subway

Although not strictly part of the Underground System, the Tower Subway was the world's first underground tube railway. Constructed using the revolutionary Greathead Shield invented by James Henry Greathead (used subsequently for many of the other tubes), the train (actually a single carriage) was cable operated and was effectively used as a shuttle service between the two banks of the Thames.

The railway, unfortunately, was only open from August 2nd 1870 until November the same year due to very poor patronage.

It cost back then 2d for 1st Class who had priority boarding or 1d for second class. Its drop-in usage led to the company's bankruptcy and the tunnel reverted to a foot tunnel charging 1/2d and was used a great deal until the opening of the Tower Bridge Walkway in 1897, which saw the start of demise of the foot tunnel, in fact a year later it was sold to the London Hydraulic Power Company.

So back to Tower Hill, and then turn left onto Byward Street walk past the Church All Hallows by the Tower, this site has had a church here for over 1300 years, and it was here that it is believed that Samuel Pepys also saw the Great fire of London from the churches tower.

Straight on and you will see the next pub the Hung Drawn and Quartered on the right.

The Hung Drawn and Quartered

Address: 26-27 Great Tower St, London EC3R 5AQ
Phone: 020 7626 6123
Nearest Tube: Tower Hill
Hours:

Saturday	9am–11pm
Sunday	9am–6pm
Monday	9am–11pm
Tuesday	9am–11pm
Wednesday	9am–11pm
Thursday	9am–11pm
Friday	9am–11pm

- A watering hole from whence you can survey the Tower and Execution Site. Refurbished in 2015, which offers a brief respite before moving on. Check out the plaques/paintings on the wall for some local information.
- While for many Tower Green inside the Tower of London is synonymous with beheadings, only seven people, including Anne Boleyn, were ever actually executed there. Far more people were

executed outside the Tower's walls at nearby Tower Hill, just up the road.

- Some of the names of those executed here are recorded on a memorial at the site – everyone from Simon Sudbury, the Archbishop of Canterbury who was beheaded here by an angry mob in 1381, through to Sir Thomas More in 1535 (gracious King Henry VIII commuted his sentence from being hung, drawn and quartered to mere beheading), and Simon Fraser, the 11th Lord Lovat, a Jacobite arrested after the Battle of Culloden and the last man to be executed here when his head was lopped off in 1747.

- While, as you can see above, many of those executed at Tower Hill were beheaded (and most were of the nobility), there were some executions there which did involve the guilty party being hung, drawn and quartered – a punishment reserved for those being convicted of high treason and also enforced at other sites in London including at Tyburn and Smithfield. Among them was William Collingbourne in 1484 for supporting the cause of Henry Tudor against that of King Richard III.

A plaque on the external wall of the nearby pub quotes a passage from the famous diarist Samuel Pepys after he witnessed an execution in Charing Cross on 13th October, 1660: "I went to see Major General Harrison. Hung drawn and quartered. He was looking as cheerful as any man could in that condition". Thomas Harrison fought with Parliament during the Civil War and was among those who signed the death warrant of King Charles I. Found guilty of regicide after the Restoration, he was hung, drawn and quartered (though as Pepys tells us, "not here"). *https://exploring-london.com/2014/07/21/london-pub-signs-the-hung-drawn-and-quartered*

Route: When you exit the pub head towards Westminster taking Lower Thames Street. Continue until you reach Fish Street Hill on your right, which will lead you to our last pub in this crawl. En route you will find a few interesting sites.

You will past Custom house on the left. Until 1814 the Custom House stood in the parish of All Hallows Barking, immediately to the east of the present site.

- The site was long known as "Wool Quay", and, from the medieval period, a custom house was necessary there to levy the duty payable on exported wool. Such a building is recorded as early as 1377. The quay and the buildings on it were privately owned. Around 1380, one John Churchman built a custom house there to collect dues for the City of London, and in 1382 the crown came to an agreement to use its facilities.

- Churchman's custom house remained in use until 1559, the freehold passing through various hands. Its replacement was erected under the direction of William Paulet, Marquess of Winchester, the Lord High Treasurer. A print from 1663 shows it as a three-storey building, with octagonal staircase towers. This structure was destroyed in the Great Fire of 1666.

- The post-fire replacement was on a rather larger scale, to the designs of Christopher Wren. The original estimate was for £6,000, but the eventual cost was more than £10,000. The new building was short- lived: in January 1715 a fire, which began in a nearby house, damaged the it beyond repair, and a new, larger structure was built to the designs of Thomas Ripley, "Master-Carpenter" to the board of Customs. This necessitated the acquisition of ground to the north, fronting onto Thames Street, and the east. The main body of the new building, however, had the same plan as Wren's, and may have re-used its foundations, but was of three, rather than two storied.

Carrying on down the road we next come to Old Billingsgate Market, this is the name given to what is now a hospitality and events venue in the City of London, based in the Victorian building that was originally Billingsgate Fish Market, the world's largest fish market in the 19th century.

- The first Billingsgate Market building was constructed on Lower Thames Street in 1850 by the builder John Jay, and the fish market was moved off the streets into its new riverside building. This was demolished in around 1873 and replaced by an arcaded market hall designed by City architect Horace Jones and built by John Mowlem & Co. in 1875, the building that still stands on the site today.

- In 1982, the fish market itself was relocated to a new site on the Isle of Dogs in east London. The 1875 building was then refurbished by architect Richard Rogers, originally to provide office accommodation.

- The Market rights of the City of London were based on a charter granted by Edward III in 1327 which prohibited the setting up of rival markets within 6.6 miles of the City, (six and two thirds miles being the distance a person could be expected to walk to market, sell his produce and return in a day). In 1400 King Henry IV granted to the citizens the right, by charter, to collect tolls and customs at Billingsgate, Cheap and Smithfield. Since then, various Acts have confirmed the City's role as the Market Authority and laid down its responsibilities and rights, including the making of regulations, the collection of tolls, rents and other charges.

- Billingsgate was known as Blynesgate and Byllynsgate before the name settled into its present form. The origin of the name is unclear and could refer to a watergate at the south side of the City where goods landed.
- Billingsgate was originally a general market for corn, coal, iron, wine, salt, pottery, fish and miscellaneous goods and does not seem to have become associated exclusively with the fish trade until the 16th century.
- In 1699 an Act of Parliament was passed making it "a free and open market for all sorts of fish whatsoever". The only exception to this was the sale of eels which was restricted to Dutch fishermen whose boats were moored in the Thames. This was because they had helped feed the people of London during the Great Fire.

Next, we come across the Church St Magnus the Martyr on the left. Worth putting you head in to see this church which has been on this site since the 1100s. Also, it has a model of London Bridge and how it looked when it was filled with houses.

- The church has a chequered history in that it just missed damage in an earlier great fire in 1633, which destroyed 42 premises on the northern third of London Bridge and a further eighty buildings on Thames Street. Some of these buildings were not repaired or replaced, and this accidental "firebreak" prevented the bridge from being damaged by the Great Fire of London three decades later in September 1666.
- Despite its escape in 1633, the church was one of the first buildings to be destroyed in the Great Fire of London in 1666. St Magnus stood less than 300 yards from the bakehouse of Thomas Farriner in Pudding

Lane where the fire started. Farriner, a former churchwarden of St Magnus, was buried in the middle aisle of the church on 11 December 1670, perhaps within a temporary structure erected for holding services.

But before going in for our last libation a quick detour to the Monument itself.

- The Monument, on Fish Street Hill in the City of London, commemorates the 1666 Great Fire of London and at 61.5m (202 feet) is the tallest free-standing stone column in the world.
- Designed by Sir Christopher Wren on the orders of King Charles II the Monument was completed in 1677. The Portland stone column has a gilt-bronze flaming urn on top and seems to shine on even the dullest of days.
- Wren's original plan was to place a statue of the King Charles II on top, but the Monarch rejected the plans by reportedly stating, 'I did not start the fire!'
- The Great Fire, which started in a baker's shop in Pudding Lane exactly 202 feet (61.5m) away from the Monument, destroyed 80% of the City of London's medieval buildings including St Paul's Cathedral.
- Fanned by a strong wind, the fire raged through the City's densely packed wooden buildings for over five days.
- It was finally brought under control by soldiers based at the Tower of London barracks who, took advantage of the drop in winds speed, and forced fire breaks by blowing up the buildings in front of the fire.
- Although over 70,000 people's homes, 87 churches, 44 halls, The Royal Exchange and Customs House &

St Pauls Cathedral were all destroyed there were only six verified deaths.

- "In the immediate aftermath of the fire, a poor demented French watchmaker called (Lucky) Hubert, confessed to starting the fire deliberately: justice was swift and he was rapidly hanged. It was sometime later however that it was realised that he couldn't have started it, as he was not in England at the time!" *http://www.historic-uk.com/HistoryUK/HistoryofEngland/The-Great-Fire-of-London/*

- Only six people died in the Great Fire of London, but seven people died by falling or jumping from the Monument before a safety rail was built.

So to our last pub, travel back down on Fish Street Hill until you reach the monument pub on the right.

The Monument

Address: 18 Fish St Hill, London EC3R 6DB
Phone: 020 7929 5880
Nearest Tube: Monument
Hours:

Saturday	11am–6:30pm
Sunday	11am–6:30pm
Monday	11am–11pm
Tuesday	11am–11pm
Wednesday	11am–11pm
Thursday	11am–11:30pm
Friday	11am–11:30pm

Nothing of note, history wise about this pub, just a very nice place to finish off the crawl.

The start of our next Crawl starts over on the South Side of the River Thames which can be accessed via London Bridge, if you feel up to it come out of the pub and

turn left onto Monument Street, at the junction turn left onto London Bridge and cross over to the South Side!

So that concludes this crawl, as we progress onto the next one we will delve into an area filled with prostitutes and smugglers, but before we head off;
Below is a taster about London Bridge!

London Bridge:

- The first stone built bridge over the Thames was in 1136, and soon after houses were starting to be built on the bridge, and these stayed there as part of the substance of the bridge until the mid-18th century. It also remained the only way to cross the river (unless you took a ferry) until 1727 when Putney Bridge was built, and soon after in 1738 Westminster Bridge became the third bridge.

- London Bridge has become synonymous with London across the globe thanks to the song 'London Bridge is falling Down', in fact some visitors today still believe that Tower Bridge is London Bridge, and I suppose if your visiting from another country your preconceptions could lead you to make that supposition, as all the tourist information shows Tower Bridge as an icon of London.

- Parts of London Bridge collapsed on various occasions throughout history, including 1282, 1309, 1425 and 1437. The 1282 collapse happened when expanding ice from the frozen Thames crushed five of the arches. Queen Eleanor, who was not a very popular Monarch at the best of times, was blamed for re-assigning bridge revenues thereby failing to use them to upkeep the bridge. This gave rise to a populous version of the rhyme "London Bridge is falling down": the original was based around an old Norse saga, but the new version included "my fair lady" was a slight at the Queen.

Alongside the normal historic facts/legends/lore here are a few lesser known ones.

- After the Great Fire in 1666, people tended to drift away from the city as it became a less fashionable place to live, and by the 18th century Old London Bridge became synonymous with 'congestion!' (Maybe they should have had a congestion charge back then!) What with the houses, some seven stories high, the drawbridge, the waterwheels etc. traffic had very little space, and although the bridge was 8m wide in some places due to houses etc. it was reduced to just about 4m, and it could take about an hour to cross.

- In an effort to improve the situation The City decided to introduce a new Rule, requiring traffic should keep to the left, this important decision played no small part in the Highways Bill 1835, where this concept was formalised. Despite this, after the other bridges opened London Bridge lost some of its appeal, so in an attempt to improve the situation further all houses were to be removed, and this work was completed in 1760.

- Up until the 1660s traitors' heads were set on spikes on Old London Bridge. The first man to have his tar-soaked head displayed in this manner was Scottish freedom fighter William Wallace, in 1305. This practice continued until the 1660s approx. and included the heads of Thomas More, Guy Fawkes and Oliver Cromwell.

- Old London Bridge was the longest inhabited bridge in the world and drew tourists in from around the world.
- In the 1960s Old London Bridge was falling down! So what could they do! One bright spark had the idea of selling it, and use the funds to build a new one, but who would buy it…? You guessed it, an American by the name Robert P McCullock, who had it dismantled and shipped to Arizona where it was used to face a new concrete bridge. Folklore suggests that he may have been duped and thought he was buying Tower Bridge, however there is no proof of this.
- Fire was another hazard of life on the bridge. The worst fire started in 1212 when sparks and embers from a house fire at the Southwark end travelled across the Thames and started another fire at the north end. Those people trapped in the middle jumped from the bridge into waiting rescue boats, sinking many of them or into the Thames itself. It's estimated that at least 3,000 people lost their lives that day. This became known as the Great Fire of Southwark, and is probably London's greatest ever peace time disaster.
- An original half domed stone alcove erected in the 1760s now stands in the grounds of Guys hospital.

Race for Doggett's Coat and Badge

- Thomas Doggett was an actor who played comedy parts in the 1700s and became associated with the management of the Theatre Royal, Haymarket and the Drury Lane Theatre. A confirmed 'whig' and supported the crown, in fact he organised this race in commemoration of King George 1's ascension to the Throne in 1714.

- The race was to be a competition between 'only young watermen' who were in their first year of their apprenticeship, of the 'Freedom of the Watermen's Company', however as time marched on and the need for 'watermen' declined, Doggett's custom had to be expanded and so by 1988, a person could enter three times.

"The Doggett's Race is held each summer on the Thames, between London Bridge and Cadogan Pier (Chelsea) – the sites of the Old Swan Tavern and the Swan Inn Chelsea. Up to six young watermen will row under 11 bridges on the 4-mile 7-furlong (7,400 metre) course. Throughout its 300-year history the race has remained relatively unchanged. However, until 1873, competitors rowed against the tide using four-seater passenger wherries and there are stories of the race taking over two hours to complete. Since then the race has been rowed with the tide and the passenger wherries have been replaced by modern sculling boats. The time now taken to complete the course is between 25 to 30 minutes and in 1973 Bobby Prentice, now Bargemaster to the Fishmongers' Company and Upper Warden of the Company of Watermen and Lightermen, set the fastest recorded time of 23 minute 22 seconds" http://www.doggettsrace.org.uk/about-the-race/ *(2016)*

Crawl Number 2
London Bridge to Blackfriars South of River: Southwark Etc. (Bishop's Geese to Jerusalem)

South of the River Thames, a really strange thing in my experience, from the people I know, those who live north of the blue line on the map, would not want to move south, and similarly those who live south would not dream of moving north! Now being a southerner of course I can wax lyrical about the South, suffice to say that during the history of this city, all the entertainment (prostitution, gambling, drinking & cock fighting etc.) all went on in the South as you will see on this crawl.

So in the wisdom of Benjamin Franklin:

"Beer is proof that God loves us and wants us to be happy."

Pubs on Route: (Approximately 1.7 miles)

The Old Thameside Inn – Globe Tavern – The Old Kings Head – The George Inn – The Market Porter – The Anchor – The Swan Shakespeare's Globe

Starting Point:

Old Thameside Inn

Address: Pickfords Wharf, Clink St, London SE1 9DG
Phone: 020 7403 4243
Nearest Tube: London Bridge
Hours:

Monday	10am–11:30pm
Tuesday	10am–11:30pm
Wednesday	10am–11:30pm
Thursday	10am–11:30pm
Friday	10am–12am
Saturday	10am–11:30pm
Sunday	10am–11pm

- This pub has a major tourist attraction right next door, a replica of Francis Drakes, Golden Hinde in which he sailed around the world.
- The new Golden Hinde has also clocked up over 100,000 miles since her launch in 1973. Despite the

pubs name it is fairly new being opened in 1895. Its history, is that it was once a spice warehouse and was very busy due to being ideally located next to the Thames, however, over time business dwindled and it fell into ruin until it was renovated. Now a thriving pub with a great riverside location. Tourists flock to the area, not only for the Golden Hinde, but for The Clink museum which is just around the corner, and the Globe Theatre (where we end this crawl).

Route: Coming out of the Old Thameside Inn, turn right into Clink Street and follow to the end.

- Here you come across the Clink Museum, sited on the original grounds of the Clink prison which dates back to 1144 and was one of England's most notorious and oldest prisons. What you need to be aware of is that back then London was a different place, and the laws were set by the areas in which you lived. As such this area south of the Thames was not governed by the City of London, but rather by the Bishop of Winchester! Confused?

Let me try and explain.

- This area was known as The **Liberty of the Clink**, sitting on the south bank of the River Thames, opposite the City of London. Although situated in Surrey, as it was back then the liberty was exempt from the jurisdiction of the county's high sheriff and was under the jurisdiction of the Bishop of Winchester who was usually either the Chancellor or Treasurer of the King.

- But back in 1129 it was Henry de Blois, King Stephen's brother, and 'Billy the Bastard's' grandson (that's William the Conqueror for those that have visited his home town of Falaise in France) who was invested as the Bishop of Winchester, and second in power to the King.

- His Thameside residence, Winchester Palace was completed in 1144 and contained two prisons within the palace grounds: one for men, and one for women.
- So Bankside as it was known became subject to the laws of 'The Liberty (or jurisdiction) of the Bishop of Winchester' (later the 'Liberty of The Clink') and was run accordingly. (We will talk more about the Bishop of Winchester later on in this crawl, interesting point though, before all this went on in the 12th Century, back in the 9th Century St Swithun was a Bishop of Winchester!)
- Suffice to say, that as this area was not under the auspices of the City of London, this area became 'an entertainment centre' for London, all run by the Bishop!

Some of the 'entertainment included:

Prostitution

- In 1161 the bishop was granted the power to license prostitutes and brothels in the liberty. The prostitutes were known as Winchester Geese, and many are buried in Cross Bones (we will see this site later), an unconsecrated graveyard. Some sayings started from here, i.e. to "be bitten by a Winchester goose" meant "to catch a venereal disease", and "goose bumps" was slang for symptoms of venereal diseases.
- In tune with the entertainment on offer, brothels were plentiful, known as stews (originally "stew" meant a fish pond, then attributed to a public bath-house, and eventually a common name for a brothel), often

painted white and facing the Thames, with their signs painted on the walls so that customers who were ferried across the Thames could easily locate their favourite!

Theatres

- Theatres and playhouses were allowed in the Clink, the most famous being the Globe Theatre. Another noted one was The Rose, where Shakespeare and Christopher Marlowe both premiered plays.

Animal baiting

- Bull and bear baiting were also allowed. And reference to this is made by Samuel Pepys in his diaries "The Bear Garden was situated on bankside close to the precinct of the Clinke Liberty and very near to the old palace of the bishops of Winchester"
- The first animal-baiting pit on Bankside was probably built at the turn of the 15th Century or so. No precise record has been found. The last one to be shut down was approximately a hundred or so years later. It's worth noting that this atrocious 'entertainment' was however, not banned until 1835.

Back to the Clink!

- Spanning for over 600 years, it witnessed a huge amount of social, economic and political change in England, and as such 'hosted' a plethora of sinners throughout its tenure, including debtors, heretics, drunkards, harlots, and later religious zealots.

Ghost Alert

As you can image the pain and suffering which went on within the wall of this prison must have been horrendous! They even do Ghost hunts here today. As so many people met their end here it is not possible to put a name to any of the ghosts/hauntings which have happened here, suffice to say if you wish to be brave, wander the area when its quiet at night, and see what happens! (DO NOT BE ON YOUR OWN!)

Route: Head down Stoney Street and turn left into Winchester Walk then right into Cathedral Street. (In front of you is Southwark Cathedral.)

Southwark Cathedral: **(or the Cathedral and Collegiate Church of St Saviour and St Mary Overie).** (Worth a quick dignified look!)

- Word of mouth suggests that there was a community of Nuns living here prior to the Norman Invasion in the 7th century, so a building of religious significance has been on this site for nearly 1400 years.
- There some evidence that Swithun, Bishop of Winchester in the 9th century, changed the convent to a college of priests. The first written reference of a 'minster' here in Southwark was in the Domesday Book (1086).

"In 1106 the church was 're-founded' by two Norman knights as a priory, living according to the rule of St Augustine of Hippo, dedicated to St Mary and later known as St Mary Overy ('over the river'). Like most of the surrounding area, Southwark was under the care of the bishops of Winchester, and much of the building's future would depend on the goodwill of the bishops who lived in a palace just west of the church. The Augustinians created a hospital alongside the church, the direct predecessor of today's St Thomas's

Hospital opposite the Houses of Parliament and originally named in honour of St Thomas Becket." (*http://cathedral.southwark.anglican.org/visit/history-and-architecture*)

A quick fact:

The bells at the Cathedral number 12 in all, and the heaviest, or "Tenor", is in the top ten of the heaviest change-ringing bells in existence. It weighs in at nearly two and a half tons.

Strange but True?

The Rich Ferryman of Southwark: (John Overy The Miser of Southwark);

"According to legend, John Overs ran a ferry east of London Bridge. Despite making plenty of money he was loth to spend it. He even pretended to die, expecting his household to fast in mourning, thus saving him the cost of feeding them for 24 hours. However, his abused servants were glad to see the end of him, broke into the pantry and had a party. Overs jumped from his 'deathbed' to complain, scared the life out of his servants who mistook him for a ghost, and got brained with an oar. His daughter Mary, distraught at her father's death, sent a message to her lover to come to comfort her. Such was his excitement at sharing the large inheritance that he rode his horse too quickly, was thrown off and died as well. Believing herself cursed, Mary joined a convent, using the ferry fortune to build a church, called St Mary Overies, where Mary is buried."

(*http://www.grosvenorprints.com/stock_detail.php?ref=4517*)

Ghost Alert

It is not beyond the wit of man to realise that if ghosts frequent this life's plane because they are tormented souls, then this poor fellow who was mistaken for a ghost would have just cause to come back and deliver some 'pay back!' Back on to the next watering hole:

Route: carry on down Cathedral Street, which becomes Beadle Street and pass under the railway arch where you will find the Globe Tavern on the left.

The Globe Tavern

Address: 8 Bedale St, London SE1 9AL
Phone: 020 7407 0043
Nearest Tube: London Bridge
Hours:

Monday	11am–11pm
Tuesday	11am–11pm
Wednesday	11am–11pm
Thursday	11am–11pm
Friday	11am–12am
Saturday	11am–12am
Sunday	12–10:30pm

- Right in the heart of Borough Market this pub dates from 1872, built in a Gothic revival style by Henry Jarvis. It has featured in two films – Blue Ice (Michael Caine) and more recently Bridget Jones's Diary. The pub is steeped in history and as the plaque on the front of the pub states. It was actually named after the Globe Theatre and for some time it was believed that Shakespeare's Globe Theatre had actually stood on this very site... but no! Seems that they got that all wrong, but the name stuck.

Borough Market;

It appears that there has been a Market of some sort here for over 1000 years. The earliest reference that can be found is from the writings of Snorri Sturluson, who in his tales of Olaf (later King of Norway and Saint), but at this time was a Viking mercenary working for Ethelred the Unready, who was trying to depose Canute, after Canute's father had died, and chose to hire scary and violent Vikings to do his work and this was in 1014.

In the saga Heimskringla, the first paragraph states

- "First they made their way to London, and so up into the Thames, but the Danes held the city. On the other side of the river is a great market town called Southwark..." *(http://boroughmarket.org.uk/history)*

There is a lot written about the history of Borough Market, who owned it, when it open what it sold, but a few lesser known facts are as follows.

- The area gets its name from a time when it was the only borough outside the City of London. Beyond the jurisdiction of the City authorities, in the 16th and 17th centuries the area was a playground famed for its inns, theatres and the notorious Southwark Fair which was shut down in 1762 after being deemed too debauched.

- The market went from strength to strength before eventually being closed by an act of parliament in the 18th Century due to it causing too much congestion on the street. When this happened, Southwark residents were granted permission to start a new market away from the road by way of compensation. In 1756 a group of locals launched Borough Market in its current location and it slowly built up to become one of London's most important food markets.

- Nearby pub, The Market porter (not on our crawl but a nice pub if you're in need of a slight diversion, nice food as well) is reportedly haunted. Supposedly in the late 1800s a local marketer 'Flash Alf' was brutally was stabbed to death, by his friend and companion Edward Lamb during a drunken argument outside the pub, with an umbrella! It is said they can often be seen carrying on their dispute outside the pub late at night!

Back to business of our crawl about Southwark.

Route: On leaving the Pub carry on down Beadle Street and turn right onto Borough High Street. Cross over and about 30-40metres down on your left you will see the arched entrance to the old Kings Head Pub

The Old Kings Head Pub

Address: King's Head Yard,
Greater London SE1 1NA
Phone: 020 7407 1550
Nearest Tube: London Bridge
Hours:

Monday	11am–12am
Tuesday	11am–12am
Wednesday	11am–12am
Thursday	11am–12am
Friday	11am–12am
Saturday	11am–12am
Sunday	11am–12am

- Practically the whole of the buildings in King's Head Yard and the houses on either side of it were destroyed by the German bombers in 1940.
- The King's Head was previously named The Pope's Head before the Reformation, and it is clearly marked on maps in the 16th century. At the start of Elizabeth

I's reign it belonged to Thomas Cure, the founder of Cure's College, and later passed to the family of Humbles.

- The King's Head was burnt down in the Borough fire of 1676. But part of the new building erected after the fire survived until 1885. Roman remains were found on the site of the inn in 1879–81 which indicated that an inhabited building had stood there during the Roman occupation. Other historical owners included St Thomas's Hospital.

The Great Fire of Southwark:

- In 1676 ten years after the Great Fire of London, another fire blighted London, this time in Southwark which destroyed upwards of 500 hundred houses, and about 20 people lost their lives. On 26th May 1676 a small fire started in Mr Welsh's paint and oil shop which was between the George Inn and the Tabard Inn, on what is now Borough High Street.
- The fire spread quickly, and it appeared that the lessons learned during the Great Fire of London ten years earlier had not yet reached Southwark. The fire engine pipes were old, punctured and of little use.
- Southwark was still made up of old timber-framed buildings and narrow streets.
- Without the firefighting equipment, the fire raged for 17 hours and was only extinguished when they removed fuel from the fires path by blowing up houses to create a fire break as they had done in the Great Fire of London some ten years earlier.
- Yet again, King Charles II and his brother the Duke of York assisted in the fire-fighting effort.

The Tabbard Inn was rebuilt following the fire but was later demolished in the 19th century.

Onto our next establishment, which was rebuilt following the fire.

Route: As you come out of Kings Head Yard turn left and travel about 75 yards down the road until you reach the Arch for the George Pub on your left.

The George Inn

Address: 75-77 Borough High Street, Southwark, SE1 1NH
Phone: 0207 407 2056
Nearest Tube: London Bridge
Hours:
Mon- Sat: 11:00 -23:00
Sun: 12:00 -22.30

- The earliest reference to the George Inn is shown on a map dated 1542, held at the public records office. It is also known that the George Inn was well established during the reign of Henry VIII. And the first known landlord/innkeeper was a man named Nicholas Marten in 1558.
- In John Stowe's 'Survey of London' dated 1598, he makes reference to the George Inn as 'one of the eight fair inns'.

- Following the fire which destroyed the pub, in 1677 the pub was once again open for business. And some of the original building still stands today.

- The George was one of the many coaching inns in those days, and those with galleries were the precursor to the original theatres. Shows were performed to the delight of the customers who were very near to the players, they would perform on a 'stage' in the Courtyard with some of the audience in front of them, (this area was known as the pit, possibly after the Elizabethan cock pits, which were also 'muddy' areas) and those who paid a premium price would be up in the Galleries and have better, more comfortable view.

- These galleries provided an excellent viewing platform and it is believed that this 'set up' was the reason why our theatres today have galleries, stalls, and a pit. As theatres were built and they took the performances inside and moved away from the courtyards, it was a natural progression to keep the same names so as 'customers' were comfortable the usual terms. This can be seen in the Globe, which we will visit later on this crawl.

- Later on in its history the author Charles Dickens apparently used to relax in the George and even made reference to it in his book, _Little Dorrit_. 'Tip goes into the George to write begging letters'.

- 'By 1844, Frances Scholefield had taken over the inn (widow of the late Westerman Scholefield). The coming of the railways that had begun threatening the coaching trade had reached Southwark, creating London Bridge Station. Despite the coming of the railways, the inn continued to be busy, and on the night of the 1851 census 15 people were staying there. The clientele included a sailor, an architect, a commercial traveller, two waggoners and a customs house clerk, as well as the resident inn staff.' *http://www.traveldudes.org/travel-tips/george-inn-southwark-historical-pub-london/11420*

- However, as the railways started taking a foot hold and coach travel diminished, a large portion of The George Inn was knocked down by the Great Northern Railway to create space for warehouses, leaving only parts of the south face intact.
- Today the pub is owned/managed by the National Trust which is unusual in itself, but adds to the air of authenticity present through its timbered frame. Its galleries at the front of the building, are the last still in existence in London. Timber framed buildings have inherent risk from fire, so many of the other surviving examples were destroyed during the Blitz in Second World War's aerial bombardment (The Blitz).

Ghost Alert

This pub reputedly has a spectre of an old women who moves about the upstairs, checking in on the customers. Thought to be the old landlady Mrs Murray, it also has a penchant for messing with electrical items, although when checked they appear in working order!

Just outside back in 1855, a man who can only be described as 'eccentric!' committed suicide by hanging himself in the yard, no one knows why, but it appears the soul is not at rest as he still frequents the premises today!

Route: Back on to Borough High Street and we turn left and head down towards Borough Tube station. As we

get to the junction of Marshalsea Road and Borough High Street you will see a church on the left, St George the Martyr. Cross over and continue into Marshalsea Road. Take second right into Redcross Way. Continue along Redcross Way until the junction with Southwark Street. Turn right and then take the first left into Stoney Street, and the Market Porter is up on your left.

A bit of a walk until the next pub, but there are few bits history you may not have seen in your history books on the way. (But the next two pubs are very close!)

On your route:

St George: The Martyr Church

At first glance, the tower of St George The Martyr looks like any other church tower. Indeed, it has four sides, on each one of which is displayed a handsome clock face. One face for each point of the compass.

So, nothing really out of the ordinary.

- But, look closer at the dial that is east facing! Can you spot the difference between this face and the other 3? The other three clocks have white faces and are illuminated at night, whereas this one has a black face and isn't. A popular belief for this strange phenomenon has to do with the church's rebuilding, which took place between 1734 and 1736.

- Local residents were asked to contribute financially towards the building of the new church and those who were living in each surrounding district dug deep into their pockets to pay for the construction – with the notable exception of the people of the district of Bermondsey, situated to the east of the church.

- No one really knows why they did not contribute, but whatever their reasons, it was decided that, if Bermondsey had no time for St George, then St George would, quite literally, have no time for Bermondsey. So, the side of the tower that faced towards Bermondsey was left blank. Sometime later the church authorities had a change of heart and added a clock face on the side of the tower that faced to the east.

- However, unwilling to completely let bygones be bygones, they coloured it black as a timely reproach.

  http://www.uncoveringlondon.co.uk/st-george-the-martyr-clock.htm

- Information from the 'uncovering London' website also tells of the stained glass window inside the church which depicts Little Dorrit from the Charles Dickens novel of the same name. See some extracts below.

- Charles Dickens was first to use St George the Martyr in 1824 when his father, John Dickens, was locked up for debt in Marshalsea Prison which was just next door.

- Dickens wrote his book Little Dorrit (known in the book as the Child of Marshalsea) in 1856, and because the Church stood next to the prison, it appears to have been a main source of inspiration.

- The prison and the church feature quite prominently, throughout the book, and a homage to these references can be seen within a stained glass window in the church. If you walk up towards the altar and look up at the stained glass window behind it, and examine the left panel you will see the figure of St George, sword in hand. Follow the line of the sword and you see will its pointing to scroll of paper being stood on by his left foot.

This is Little Dorrit and, although she might not be "as large as life", she is most certainly still, very much, one of the curiosities of the lovely church of St George the Martyr. *http://www.uncoveringlondon.co.uk/little-dorrits-church.htm*

Cross Bones Graveyard:

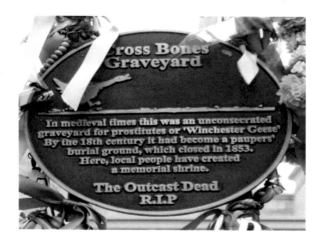

- There are large gates are covered with, ribbons, flowers, feathers, etc. – and a bronze tablet which says: 'R.I.P. The Outcast Dead'. This is Cross Bones Graveyard a burial ground with a historic links dating back to the medieval times.
- In his 1598 Survey of London, the historian John Stow refers to a burial ground for 'single women' – a euphemism for the prostitutes who worked in Bankside's brothels or 'stews'. Stow writes:
- 'I have heard of ancient men, of good credit, report that these single women were forbidden the rites of the church, so long as they continued that sinful life, and were excluded from Christian burial, if they were not reconciled before their death. And therefore there was a plot of ground called the Single Woman's churchyard, appointed for them far from the parish church.'
- From the 12th to the 17th century, the Bishop of Winchester was effectively the Lord of this manor,

'the Liberty of the Clink', in Southwark, which we referenced earlier on in this crawl where we saw the site of his London residence. Many nefarious activities which were forbidden within the City walls were permitted and regulated within the Liberty, and were under control of the Bishop.

- By Shakespeare's time, this stretch south of the river was known as London's pleasure quarter, with theatres, bear-pits, taverns and brothels – these 'stews', licensed by the Bishop under Ordinances dating from 1161 and signed by Thomas Becket. In life, such women (known as the Bishops of Winchesters Geese) enjoyed a measure of protection from the church; in death, if John Stow is to be believed, they were denied even a Christian burial.

- This then is the reason why this Graveyard (also known back then as the Single Women's Churchyard) came about. Having plied their trade for the Bishop one would have thought that they had the church's blessing, but no! If they had not repented their ways by the time they had died, they died in a state of sin, and could not be buried on consecrated grounds.

- Yet still today the ladies which were buried here are remembered by many who keep coming back to lay their flowers, ribbons etc.

"I was born a Goose of Southwark
By the Grace of Mary Overie
Whose Bishop gives me licence
To sin within the Liberty."

(The Southwark Mysteries: J Constable)

The Market Porter

Address: 9 Stoney St, London SE1 9AA
Phone: 020 7407 2495
Hours:

Sunday	12–10:30pm
Monday	6–8:30am, 11am–11pm
Tuesday	6–8:30am, 11am–11pm
Wednesday	6–8:30am, 11am–11pm
Thursday	6–8:30am, 11am–11pm
Friday	6–8:30am, 11am–11pm
Saturday	12–11pm

The Market Porter has an envious location in a historic district of London and even boasts a link to the people who Love Harry Potter as the pub was transformed into the 'Third Hand Book Emporium' in the film 'Harry Potter and the Prisoner of Azkaban', and was situated next to 'The Leaky Cauldron.

There has been a pub on this site since at least 1638, and was previously addressed at 25 Borough Market in 1868 &

earlier; the current building dating from the 1890s. It is now called the Market Porter.

Ghost Alert

It is believed that in the late 1800s a local marketer 'Flash Alf' was killed by being stabbed to death, with an umbrella, outside this pub. That night a row had erupted between Alf and his friend/companion Edward Lamb, after a beer fuelled night on the town. As they were friends before this event maybe it's these two fellows that are often seen in shadows at bar by passers by late at night after the pub has closed, making up their differences!

Other issues have included a landlord who said he had shut of the glass washer, only to awake the next morning with it switched on and the pub floor flooded!

Route: Turn left into Park Street and follow until the fork with Bank End. Bear right into Bank End and continue until the river front whereupon you will see the Anchor pub on your left.

The Anchor Pub

Address: 34 Park St, Southwark,
London SE1 9EF
Phone: 020 7407 1577
Nearest Tube: London Bridge
Hours:

Monday	11am–12am
Tuesday	11am–11pm
Wednesday	11am–11pm
Thursday	11am–12am
Friday	11am–12am
Saturday	12–11pm
Sunday	12–11pm

The first official record of the Anchor was made in 1822, however, other records tell of a more macabre past. As well as being the site of a Roman grave and a venue that held bear and bull baiting pits, the site on which the Anchor lies was also allegedly used for plague pits during 1603.

- It was most likely that the Anchor owes its name to an early owner of the brewery, Josiah Childs, who gave the pub its current name in 1665. Childs was closely involved with the navy, to whom he supplied 'Masts, Spars and Bowsprits as well as stores and small beer'. At one time the locals referred to this pub as 'Thrales of Deadman's place', as 'Thrales' referred to the brewery at the time". *http://www.taylor-walker.co.uk/pub/anchor-bankside-southwark/p0977/*

- This pub is the sole survivor of the riverside inns that existed here in Shakespeare's time when this district was at the heart of theatre land and the Thames was London's principal highway. It was frequented by many actors from the neighbouring playhouses, including the Globe, the Swan and the Rose.

- It is where diarist Samuel Pepys saw the Great Fire of London in 1666. He wrote that he took refuge in "a little alehouse on bankside ... and there watched the fire grow". Another fire, probably the Great Fire of Southwark in 1676, devastated the pub whose interior was mainly of wooden construction. It was rebuilt almost straight way and has since has had many additions and make-overs throughout the centuries.

- The Anchor tavern became a favoured haunt for pirates and smugglers, who used the Thames, mainly due to its riverside location: Fuel to this belief was added, when in 19th century, when extensive repairs were undertaken, the extrication of a massive oak beam revealed cleverly hidden cubby holes, which were probably used to store contraband etc.

Ghost Alert:

Whilst sipping your beer, can you hear a dog barking? It could be the old owner's dog, who was attacked and killed whilst trying to protect his master from a 'press gang' who were keen to recruit new personnel for the navy. In ensuing fracas, the dog was badly hurt and failed to protect his master, it is believed he still frequents the pub as he has unfinished business!

Route: Walk along to the river front (Bankside) to The Swan at Shakespeare's Globe.

As you walk under Southwark Bridge some points you may find interesting.

- Although the Parliamentary Bill to construct Southwark Bridge passed in May, 1811, the actual works did not start 1813 and took six years to complete. The first stone was laid by Admiral Lord Keith on the 23rd April 1815, and the actual opening of the bridge was a big affair. On the evening of the 24th March 1819, the bridge, was illuminated with lamps, and was declared open when St Paul's Clock rang in midnight.
- Southwark Bridge was designed by John Rennie to add another route across River Thames in an attempt to reduce congestion on other crossings. The bridge was constructed of three cast-iron arches across a narrow point in the river.
- One concern however was that the additional bridge would hinder river boats using the Thames, so to allay those concerns the central arch was to be the longest span (at the time) ever made from iron, some 240 feet.

- As the Bridge was constructed using private money, a toll was put in place to recoup some money for the investors and to pay for maintenance etc.
- Unfortunately this business venture failed, people used the none toll bridges rather than pay to cross, and consequently the Bridge was sold on for a massively reduced price to the City of London, and since then in 1866, the bridge has been toll free. The Bridge was replaced in 1912 with the now present five span bridge.

Now before I take you through the Globes history, I would like you to look west towards Blackfriars Bridge, on the left you will see the Tate Modern Building, now between there and the Bridge there once stood the Albion Mills, you may well have not ever heard of these, but you may be surprised when you hear where they are referenced.

A bit of history first:

- The Albion Mills, are recognised as the 1st great factory in London. They were steam-powered mills, built in 1786 by Matthew Boulton & James Watt. What made the factory special was that it featured one of the first uses of Watt's steam engines to drive machinery. Their capacity to grind out flour was far more than windmills or watermills could do, in fact it was rumoured to start that the new mills could produce in one month what the other millers could produce in one year. Consequently, the Mills were the seen as an 'Industrial wonder' of the time.
- So much so, London's elite and tourists would travel to see them as they were a modern icon of the time. Erasmus Darwin called them *"the most powerful machines in the world."*
- What should be borne in mind that it was great for the well to do to come and see this wonder, but the

existing millers and associated workers of London saw them as a threat to their livelihood, as due to the economies of scale, they could not compete on price with the new mills.

- Attempts had been made to prevent the mills ever being built. Local millers alike had 'lobbied' City capitalists to not fund the project, but Boulton and Watt had already secured funds from elsewhere, and by 1791 it appeared the mills were turning the corner to make a profit.

  http://www.alphabetthreat.co.uk/pasttense/albionmil ls.html

- The miller's prayers seemed to have been answered when late in the evening of 2nd March 1791 people crossing Blackfriars Bridge reported seeing the glow of flames flickering through the mill's blackened windows. The fire spread quickly and within half an hour the building was completely ablaze.

- Insurer's fire engines quickly attended via the streets and on barges moored on the Thames, however due to low tide, and the east wind fuelling the fire, the building was already beyond salvation. The end of the mill came when the burning roof crashed in on itself, propelling a jet of flame into the night's sky.

- The blaze was finally put out at the start of day and London woke to find that the Albion Mills had been destroyed.

- Foul play was suspected almost immediately, not least because of the reaction with which the London mob had greeted the fire. Although no one was ever prosecuted, and later on it the cause may not have been so sinister.

- "Eventually, it was proved that this new and untested technology was in fact responsible for the mill's undoing. The young Scottish engineer John Rennie, who had worked as technical supervisor at the site since 1788, conducted an investigation into the fire and found it had been caused by an overheating baring. It transpired that the owner's claims about the profitability of the mill had been somewhat optimistic and in an effort to claw back his investment, James Wyatt had insisted on increasing both the length and rate of production. The strain pushed the mill's engines to breaking point and in the building's highly flammable atmosphere it had taken just a single spark to from the overheating machinery to spark a cataclysmic blaze."

https://theprintshopwindow.com/2013/11/15/albions-dark-satanic-mill/

So where do you know the Albion Mills from?

The hymn Jerusalem, written by William Blake, (who lived down the road from the Albion Mills at the time), mentions the 'Dark Satanic Mills' and it is widely believed it is the Albion Mills he is talking about.

"And did those feet in ancient time walk upon England's mountains green? And was the holy Lamb of God on England's pleasant pastures seen?

And did the Countenance Divine Shine forth upon our clouded hills? And was Jerusalem built here among these dark Satanic Mills?

Bring me my bow of burning gold! Bring me my arrows of desire! Bring me my spear! O clouds, unfold! Bring me my chariot of fire!" William Blake.

The Globe Theatre

- The Globe Theatre was built between 1597 and 1599 in Southwark on the south bank of London's River Thames, it was funded and built by The Lord Chamberlain's Men which was a company of actors, which included Shakespeare (he actually owned 12.5% of Globe as well) who wrote the plays for this group of actors! Indeed Shakespeare himself performed some secondary roles.
- The Globe was constructed with three stories of seating and had a capacity of up to 3000. It was basically shaped like donut with a thatched roof. Outside there was a crest depicting Hercules bearing the globe on his shoulders together with the motto
- "Totus mundus agit histrionem" (the whole world is a playhouse)
- Next to the stage was a standing area called "the pit". People who paid a penny could come and watch the shows, and these poor folk were known as "the groundlings".

- In the heat of summer, they were often mocked and labelled as the 'stinkards' by the more affluent 'seated' members of the audience! (One can only guess why!)
- In attempt to draw the audience into the theatre coloured flags were erected outside to denote the type of play being performed. The flags were Black, White or Red, and these denoted a tragedy, a comedy, or an historic play respectively.
- It is also thought the term box office came from this era, as after the start of each play the monies which were collected in boxes at the entrances were took to a room backstage to count; the box office!
- As for equality in the acting fraternity…no chance! During this period in history, there were no were no women actors! Women's roles were played by young boys as it was felt that the 'bawdy' environment of a theatrical stage was not a place for the 'more gentle sex!'
- As the theatre audience close to one another (up to 3000 people) when there were outbreaks of the Bubonic Plague the Globe Theatre was forced to close in 1603 and 1608 to try and inhibit its spread.
- At the time, the rise in popularity of theatres, and the need to attract audiences, theatres would invest in bigger and better props and costumes etc. bearing in mind there was no such thing as health and safety regulations, it was basically a free for all. And with no safety inspections, no real fire extinguishers, no public fire brigade, it would to anyone who looked at it a recipe for disaster. Now add the good idea to use live cannons (as a sound effect), and place one in the 'heavens' where there is a thatched roof! Anyone see where this is going?

- Well, lo and behold! On the 29th June 1613, during a play about Henry VIII, the cannon was fired and sparks flew into the thatched roof, and thus ensued a major blaze which according to eye witnesses completely flattened the theatre within two hours, some people say it happened even more quickly. But everyone escaped, and the only recorded event involving a man was when his trousers caught fire and was extinguished by someone by throwing a bottle of ale over them!
- After the fire, it was rebuilt a year later on the same spot. However, when the Puritans came to power they saw theatre/plays as something against their beliefs and halted all shows in 1642, and the Globe was then turned into housing. It was again rebuilt as a theatre in 1997.

To the left of the Globe Theatre as you look at it is our final stop on this crawl.

The Swan Shakespeare's Globe

Address: 21 New Globe Walk, Bankside, London, SE1 9DT
Phone: 020 7928 9444
Nearest Tube: London Bridge or Mansion House
Hours:

Monday	8am–11:30pm
Tuesday	8am–11:30pm
Wednesday	8am–11:30pm
Thursday	8am–12am
Friday	8am–12am
Saturday	10am–12am
Sunday	10am–11pm

- A new pub which has been in partnership with the Globe Theatre since 2007, indeed the pub contributes some of its revenue to the Globe Theatre trust, a charitable organisation set up to further the experience and international understanding of Shakespeare in performance.

- Overlooking the Thames, this is an ideal watering hole to finish in, and give you chance to pop immerse yourself in some culture by taking in a show in the Globe, however you may not want to labelled a stinkard, so not too many beers before the performance!
- As this finishes our crawl, if you are still feeling thirsty, and full of beans, you may want to continue on to Crawl 3, or leave it for another day. Its starting point is just around the corner!

As this was a tad short on information so little titbits to carry you over to the next Crawl.

Origins of Expressions: Have you ever wondered where or how sayings/expressions came about, well here is a few.

Under the Weather: (Feeling ill)

During a storm, going below deck rarely alleviates sea sickness, but this does not stop the person who is suffering from trying. Those who go below deck to escape the weather were usually ill and hence this expression was born.

Bring Home the Bacon (Bring in the wages)

At English Country fairs they would stage competitions to entertain the crowds. One such competition was to grease up a pig, and have people try to catch it in the quickest time. Watching men try and chase and then catch the slippery animal caused much merriment. This phrase then was coined for those who managed to catch one!

The Third Degree (A severe intense inquisition)

Whether one is aspiring to be martial arts master or a high-ranking Freemason, you need to progress through a series of proficiency tests which get progressively harder must be passed. For a Freemason to make it through to the rank of

Master Mason (Third Degree), they are subjected to a series of relentless questioning. It is easy to see why this has crossed over in to common parlance.

Dumb Blondes (a stereotype for being a bit simple!)

Countess Maria of Coventry was a blond bombshell from the 1700s. Her notoriety wasn't driven by any titillating sex scandal or on the other side of the scale by her charitable deeds. She was however famous for the amount of make-up she plastered on. Her vanity led directly to her demise as make-up in the 1700s contained high levels of lead! Eventually she died of lead poisoning, and therefore left the legacy for future women who had this look.

In Cahoots (working alongside, with someone or a group usually up to no good)

In Medieval Germany, the black forest and surrounding areas were inhabited by bandits living together in ramshackle huts known as 'Kajutes'. This cliché evolved from identifying one's association with these outlaws.

Crawl Number 3
Blackfriars to Aldwych (Monks to Knights)

A mixture of Shakespeare, Cock fighting, Ghosts, World War and Fires, what was the quote, "When a man is tired of London, he is tired of life. "Why, Sir, you find no man, at all intellectual, who is willing to leave London. No, Sir, when a man is tired of London, he is tired of life; for there is in London all that life can afford" (Samuel Johnson)

"Oh, you hate your job? Why didn't you say so? There's a support group for that. It's called EVERYBODY, and they meet at the bar." (Drew Carey)

Pubs on route: (Approximately 1.3 miles)
(Best done Monday-Friday, as some pubs close for weekend)
The Blackfriar – The Cock Pit Pub – The Viaduct Tavern – Magpie and Stump – Hoop and Grapes – < The Punch Tavern or The Old Bell Tavern > – Ye Olde Cheshire Cheese – Ye Olde Cock tavern.

Before we start drinking, just a quick note about Blackfriars.

Have you ever seen the red pillars in the Thames located just to the side of Blackfriars Road Bridge?

- Initially they were part of the original railway bridge, across the River Thames in 1864, when the London

Chatham Dover Railway was extended St Paul's Station (now longer there).

- Designed by Joseph Cubitt, it was only four tracks wide, which limited St Pauls Station capacity, so 20 years later, a second railway bridge was built next door to it to address this.
- From about 1923, suburban routes began to terminate at Waterloo and the St Paul's Bridge was becoming increasingly underused. In 1985, it was discovered that the original bridge was too weak to bear the weight of modern trains, and was dismantled just leaving the support pillars, which was handy as they were used as storage/handling areas when rebuilding the new Blackfriars station.
- Blackfriars Bridge, when opened in 1769 was the 3rd across the River Thames. It was first named after William Pitt who was Prime Minister from 1766-68 but quickly changed its name to Blackfriars, after the nearby monastery.
- Despite the quality of the stone, poor workmanship resulted in extensive damage to the bridge. Despite attempts to repair the old bridge, it was finally decided that it should be replaced. In 1869, a new bridge was opened by Queen Victoria and is the same one that stands today.
- The bridge has some elaborate stone carvings of water birds and marine life as well as a statue of Queen Victoria at the north side.

Read more: http://www.tourist-information-uk.com/blackfriars-bridge.htm#ixzz4EMWjmP1M

The Blackfriar

Address: 174 Queen Victoria St, London
EC4V 4EG
Phone: 020 7236 5474
Nearest Tube: Blackfriars
Hours:

Thursday	9am–11pm
Friday	9am–11pm
Saturday	9am–11pm
Sunday	12–10:30pm
Monday	9am–11pm
Tuesday	9am–11pm
Wednesday	9am–11pm

- Built in 1875 on the site of a medieval Dominican friary, the Blackfriar had its interior completely changed to what we see now in 1905, by the then landlord Alfred Pettit.
- The Black Friar took its name from the Dominican Friary that was in the area between 1278-1538. At the time, pubs were becoming less popular, and so complete renovations were uncommon.

- The Pub is decorated throughout with Copper art work, some denoting 'Eating fish on Friday' Carol singing', and 'Thanksgiving'. They are made from a variety of copper, plaster and marble.

"Our historic Art Nouveau Grade II masterpiece of a pub was built in 1905 on the site of a Dominican friary. The building was designed by architect H. Fuller-Clark and artist Henry Poole, both committed to the free-thinking of the Arts and Crafts Movement. Jolly friars appear everywhere in the pub in sculptures, mosaics and reliefs. We are lucky to still be here as our wonderful pub was saved from demolition by a campaign led by Sir John Betjeman and Lady Dartmouth saved the building" (from plaque outside the pub).

Route: Turn left into Queen Victoria Street, then first left into Black Friars Lane, follow on around into Playhouse Lane, then forward into Ireland Yard. At end of Ireland Yard our next stop is The Cock Pit pub.

- **Blackfriars Playhouse**
  Playhouse Yard, EC4 Tourists, visitors and just passers-by could be forgiven to overlook this place.
- Having no 'Blue plaque', of any other tourist information, it is only the name of the street, which the inquisitive may pause to think. Yet this street is one of few remaining places in London that has genuine links with Shakespeare.
- A quite street, which does not draw much attention, to itself. However, as you walk among the little alleys and yards you can imagine how it must have been back in his time.

- Blackfriars Theatre was a private theatre in 1597, and opened to the public in 1608, and it was then Burbage went into partnership with William Shakespeare, and others (forming the Lord Chamberlains Men).
- The Blackfriars Theatre held about 600-700 people and the Lord Chamberlain's Men (later the King's Men), would have performed many Shakespeare's plays either here or at, the Globe Theatre south of the River. Works of other writers were also displayed here, and even Shakespeare, who also was an actor, trod the boards on many occasions.

Ireland Yard, Blackfriars, EC4 When Shakespeare first left Stratford upon Avon to seek his fortune, he could not have foreseen his future and how he would impact on not only London, but the literary world as well.

- Apart from his literary works, he must have had a head for business, as he ended up owning properties and shares in theatres by the time of his retirement.
- Ireland Yard is probably the best documented London address of Shakespeare. Back then it was the entrance to Monastery of the Black friars. When it closed in 1538 during Henry VIII's reign when he brought about the, '*Dissolution of Monasteries*', (also referred to as the 'Suppression of the Monasteries' which was when, between 1536 and 1541 the King disbanded any Catholic premises, such as priories, monasteries etc. in his lands, sequestrated their income and sold off their assets).
- It was after this that the gatehouse was bought by Shakespeare in 1613, needing a new place to live following the Fire at The Globe.
- By this time Shakespeare was entrenched in London living, having shares in the Globe and the Blackfriars theatres, so it was a natural progression to move from

rented accommodation in Southwark to buying here near the Blackfriars Playhouse.

- Also, this part of London at the time was seen as 'the place to be', the well to do use to live north of the river and use to only cross it when they need some entertainment. Some feel that divide still exist today!
- So, with all that in mind, Shakespeare went on to pay £140 for the gate house. (See over).

"On this day in 1613, according to the surviving Deed of Conveyance, William Shakespeare bought for £140 a "dwelling house or Tenement with th'appurtenaunces situate and being within the Precinct, circuit and compasse of the late black Fryers London"

https://lostcityoflondon.co.uk/tag/blackfriars/

On our route around we passed a yard which housed some headstones. This was the site of St Ann Blackfriars and was erected in 1557, after the dissolution of the Friary. St Ann's was destroyed during the Great Fire of London 1666 after which it joined with St Andrew-by-the-Wardrobe and this site became a burial ground.

- We keep coming across 'The Wardrobe' on this walk, in fact the King's Wardrobe was a department of the royal household. Even today it's referenced in nearby Wardrobe Place and in the name of the church of St Andrew-By-the-Wardrobe.

  The King's Wardrobe, together with the Chamber, made up the personal part of medieval English government known as the King's household. Originally the room where the king's clothes, armour and treasure were stored the term was expanded to describe both its contents and the department of clerks who ran it. Early in the reign of Henry III the Wardrobe emerged out of the fragmentation of the Curia Regis to become the chief administrative and

accounting department of the Household".
https://en.wikipedia.org/wiki/Wardrobe_(governmen t)

Shakespeare died just three years after buying the Gatehouse. He bequeathed it to his daughter, (His wife had been taken care of separately), and following her death she left it to her daughter Elizabeth, who it turned out was to be Shakespeare's last blood relative. She however sold the property in about 1667.

The Cock Pit Pub

Address: 7 Saint Andrew's Hill, London
EC4V 5BY
Nearest Tube: Blackfriars
Phone: 020 7248 7315
Hours:

Thursday	11am–11pm
Friday	11am–11pm
Saturday	11am–11pm
Sunday	12–2:30pm, 7–10:30pm
Monday	11am–11pm
Tuesday	11am–11pm
Wednesday	11am–11pm

The Cockpit is a hidden gem nestled in a backstreet near St Paul's Cathedral, with a fascinating history.

- Built in the 1840s it became famed for its cockfights. Look up and you'll see the 18ft high ceiling and a balcony where punters would have watched and gambled while the cocks were cajoled into fighting for their entertainment.

- While sitting here sipping your libation, it's not hard to imagine, quite a claustrophobic/heady atmosphere when it was in full swing. However, you may be pleased to know that this barbaric sport was outlawed in 1849.
- If we travel back to Shakespeare's time, the pub would have you believe that this was the actual site of his house!
- According to the information inside the pub, the first mention of an inn on this site was in 1352, then called the 'Oakbourn Inn', situated on what would then have been the eastern edge of the Dominican friars – or 'Blackfriars' – monastery.

Onwards!

Route: Head up St Andrews Hill (passing Ireland yard on the left) then at the end of the road turn right into Carter Lane. Follow on through to Junction of Sermon Lane.

The National Firefighters Memorial

- The Firefighters Memorial is located at a symbolic site on the south side of St Paul's Cathedral in London. The Cathedral is often symbolically portrayed as a famous and iconic building which stood in defiance of all of the fires burning and general destruction around it, caused by the Blitz on London.
- The Memorial, depicting a Fire Officer and two Firemen, cast in bronze engaged in firefighting duties, was originally called 'Blitz' and was

dedicated to the men and women of the Fire Service who lost their lives as a result of their duties during World War II. Her Majesty, the late Queen Elizabeth, The Queen Mother, unveiled this memorial on 4 May 1991.

- In the year 2000 HM Government, responding to a growing feeling that a memorial to all Firefighters was long overdue, invited the Trust to consider combining such a memorial with the existing World War II 'Blitz' memorial.
- In September 2003, our Patron Her Royal Highness, The Princess Royal rededicated the newly elevated and renamed 'Firefighters Memorial'.

Route: Carry on up to St Pauls Churchyard, and go around the Cathedral clockwise following into Paternoster Row, then bear under the arch to Temple bar and straight on through Paternoster Square until the Junction of Newgate Street. Turn left into Newgate Street and follow on into Holburn Viaduct until you reach the Viaduct Tavern on the right.

St Paul's Cathedral

- St Paul's Cathedral is one of the largest churches in the world. Designed by Sir Christopher Wren, following the Great Fire of London in 1666.
- St Paul's Cathedral was the tallest building in London from its construction until 1962. The dome is the second largest in the world at 366 feet high and is reached by climbing 259 steps.
- The present cathedral was built between 1675 and 1710, however, Old St Paul's Cathedral was started by the Normans and completed by about 1240.

- One of the most well-known features of the cathedral is the Whispering Gallery. A whisper against the wall can be clearly heard at the other side, 112 feet away.
- The cathedral's crypt is the largest in Western Europe, historically.

- In 1606, four gunpowder plotters – Sir Everard Digby, Robert Winter, John Grant and Thomas Bates – were executed on 30 January 1606 in St Paul's Churchyard.
- The other four – Guy Fawkes, Thomas Winter, Ambrose Rookwood and Robert Keyes – were executed just outside Westminster Hall, in Old Palace Yard, the following day.
- In 1913, suffragettes planted a bomb under the Bishop's throne in the choir, in an effort to bring awareness to their struggle.
- World War II: Londoners had spent most of their 1940 Christmas in shelters or in underground stations. (The blitz started in September 1940 and ended in May 1941). After Christmas, there was a lull in the bombing for two nights but on 29th December the Germans returned, dropping incendiary devices etc. in the tens of thousands. Their target? The City of London.
- On 17th April 1941, the Dome completely separated from the church, just for a split second. During a bombing raid, a bomb penetrated the North Transept. The shock from the blast funnelled up into the dome and lifted the whole by a millimetre before settling back down.
- By 6.30 pm on that cold Sunday evening, the City was in flames. A US war reporter working in London at the time, messaged his office: "The second Great Fire of London has begun."
- Prime Minister Winston Churchill sent word that St Paul's Cathedral should be protected at all costs – it would boost morale to save this icon of London.

- Bombs rained down all over the city, and the Fire Service was stretched beyond peoples' imagination. (See Shoe lane later on in the crawl.)
- *Fireman Sam Chauveau was on duty that night. "By the time we finished tackling the fires on the roof of the [Stock] Exchange, the sky, which was ebony black when we first got up there, was now changing to a yellowy orange colour. It looked like there was an enormous circle of fire, including St Paul's churchyard."* http://www.bbc.co.uk/news/magazine-12016916
- The Germans did manage to get a direct hit as an incendiary device hit the roof and stayed there, however luck was on St Pauls side that night, it dislodged and fell onto the stone gallery where it was dealt with by a Fireman and a sandbag!
- Although the bombing continued across the country until May 1941, London was never hit as bad again, St Pauls survived!

Temple Bar: This arch is the ceremonial entrance to the City of London and refers to the 17th century ornamental Baroque arched gateway designed by Christopher Wren which spanned the road until its removal in 1878. Wren's arch was preserved and was re-erected in 2004 in the City.

Paternoster Row is supposed to have received its name from the fact that, when the monks of St Paul's Cathedral would process in the street chanting the Lord's Prayer, (Pater Noster is Latin for Our Father). Another suggestion is that is was named after a type of prayer bead, known as a "pater noster".

The Viaduct Tavern

Address: 126 Newgate St, London EC1A 7AA
Phone: 020 7600 1863
Nearest Tube: St Pauls
Hours:

Thursday	8:30am–11pm
Friday	8:30am–11pm
Saturday	Closed
Sunday	Closed
Monday	8:30am–11pm
Tuesday	8:30am–11pm
Wednesday	8:30am–11pm

- Built in 1869, and named after the Holburn Viaduct, (which is essentially a flyover and the first ever in central London – began in 1863 and was completed in 1869. It was considered a major architectural accomplishment, opened by Queen Victoria and is still there today.

- It replaced the Holborn Bridge that spanned the River Fleet valley as it was back then, but since then the River Fleet has been diverted underground), and is a fine and possibly last example of a 19th century Gin Palace,

(Gin Palaces: Due to the ships and the London Docks, Gin became the drink of choice in the 18th Century, even London Gin, is still a recognised Gin today, and has a different flavour to others, because of the spices. It was also sold as having medicinal benefits. So, Gin shops or 'dram shops' were set up, (originally they were chemist's because of those medicinal associations) and sold gin mostly as a take away, or to drink standing up. As the law over licensing changed these shops became larger and expanded their stock to sell ale and/or wine. In the late 1820s the first 'Gin Palaces' were built, They were based on the new fashionable shops being built at the time, fitted out at great expense and lit by gas lights. By the 1820s the popularity of these premises had increased. They began to expand and grow and because of their increased patronage, which was partly due to the atmosphere created by the ornate decorations, etched glass, decorative mirrors and gas lighting, they attracted the title of Gin Palaces).

- There is a toll booth still in place today, although originally it was used to sell beet tokens to the customers, as the place was so rough. Situated just across the road from the Old Bailey, which was the site of Newgate prison. There are even supposedly, original cells in the basement, if you can get to see them.

- However, this claim is debatable and they may have been modified to look this way, or may just be old storage rooms, but the pub's connection to Newgate Prison is accurate. Newgate was knocked down in 1902 making way for the courts of the 'Old Bailey' (which was built in 1907).

- In all probability the pub now stands on what was the original site of the Giltspur Compter, which was a debtors' prison who catered for guests from 1791 to 1853. So nowadays the pub doesn't make the claim that the cellars were part of Newgate Prison, opting for a more debatable view that they were part of the debtor's prison. However that too was demolished before the pub was built in 1869!

"Hangings were a public spectacle in the street until 1868, the year before the pub opened. The condemned would be led along Dead Man's Walk, a caged walkway between Newgate Prison and the Court. It is claimed that many were buried under the walk itself. The small water feature/fountain across the street purportedly marks the place where executions of prisoners occurred. Leading some to claim the pub is haunted by spirits in the area."
https://londonunveiled.com/2013/05/14/gin-palace/

Ghost Alert

Poltergeists are believed to be in situ here, and bar staff apparently are wary about going down in the cellar at night!

- *"1996: One manager who was cleaning the cellar on a Saturday morning reported a door slamming closed and the lights going out on him. He tried to free himself from the door but could not get out. His wife is said to have heard him and went to help him. She found that the doors were unlocked and easy to open from the outside.*

- *May 1999: Two electricians were working on the pub, moving aside carpets and tearing up floorboards. One of the men felt a tap on his shoulder a few times. The first time he dismissed it and the second time he thought his co-worker was playing a prank on him. The other worker denied tapping him. As they went back to work, they saw the heavy carpet they had rolled up get lifted into the air and dropped onto the floor." Source: Viaduct Tavern, Ghost Story*

! Detour: As we leave the pub before moving on a few points of interest to see right on the doorstep.

Route: Turn right into Giltspur Steer and carry on until the first junction on the left: Cock lane.

St Sepulchre's (The Musician's Church) Holborn Viaduct, EC1

For almost 140 years, there was a ghoulish tradition carried out here. As the result of a bequest made to St Sepulchre's in 1605, a bellman was employed to go through a tunnel which connected the church to Newgate on the night before any execution. After giving 'twelve solemn towles with double strokes' on his handbell, he would recite:

"All you that in the condemned hold do lie, Prepare you, for tomorrow you shall die; Watch all and pray, the hour is drawing near That you before the Almighty must appear; Examine well yourselves, in time repent, That you may not to eternal flames be sent: And when St Sepulchre's bell tomorrow tolls, The Lord above have mercy on your souls. Past twelve o'clock!"

These customs died out and Newgate was finally demolished in 1902 to make way for the Old Bailey but the handbell – which can only have added to the desperate misery of the jail's inhabitants – can still be seen in a case on one of the pillars in the church.
http://www.britannia.com/hiddenlondon/st_sepulchre.html

The tradition above coupled with the tolling of the twelve bells on the day of the execution is immortalised in a children's rhyme which was penned in the 1600s;

"Oranges and lemons" say the Bells of St Clement's "You owe me five farthings" say the Bells of St Martin's "When will you pay me?" say the Bells of Old Bailey "When I grow rich" say the Bells of Shoreditch

"When will that be?" say the Bells of Stepney "I do not know" say the Great Bells of Bow "Here comes a Candle to light you to Bed. Here comes a Chopper to Chop off your Head. Chip chop chip chop – the Last Man's Dead"

- The 'Bells of Old Bailey', or more precisely the tenor bell of St Sepulchre, had been used originally before Newgate Prison got its own Bell, to time the executions but after the gallows had been moved, Newgate prison (now the site of the Old Bailey) obtained its own bell.

- The history can be found on a plaque at the church which reads "The church is built on the site of an early Saxon church. Originally named St Edmund, the name was expanded to St Edmund and the Holy Sepulchre in the 12th Century while under the control of Augustinian Canons – or Knights of the Holy Sepulchre".

- The name was eventually shortened to St Sepulchre, however its official title includes the words 'without-Newgate', so titled as it lay just outside the Newgate of the now lost City Roman Wall.
- Badly damaged in the Great Fire of London in 1666, the church was rebuilt/renovated by Sir Christopher Wren's company.
- In more recent times it has become known as the Musicians church, mainly for its close association with Sir Henry Woods (famed for the Proms concerts held every year at the Royal Albert Hall) who was baptised here and had his ashes buried here following his death in 1944. As a reminder, and a tribute to his memory, every year after the proms, the wreath which is laid upon his bust at the Royal Albert Hall at the start of the promenades (the bust is borrowed every year from the Royal Academy of Music) is finally brought to St Sepulchres to be laid above his tombstone.

Cock Lane (Ghost Alert!)

- Its name may have derived from being the only place in the City where prostitutes were allowed to 'live; but conversely it may also have a less 'adult' explanation. Cock fighting was a deplorable 'sport' which was carried out in medieval times and Cock Lane probably took its name from the fact that it was the site of a breeding ground for fighting cocks.
- Cock Lane is now mainly associated with the Golden Boy (see below). However, back in the 1700s, number 33 (although now demolished), was the home of William Parsons, and was the site of a major haunting tale.

Scratching Fanny of Cock Lane!

- In 1760, William Parsons decided to take in a lodger. Mr Willian Kent moved in with his Sister in Law! Miss Fanny! (whose sister had died previously). These lovers were quite content at Number 33, and at some time Mr Kent lent Mr Parsons some money, however he did not seem keen to make the repayments and so a tension grew between the two men.

- At this time Mr Kent had to leave for a time on business matters, which left Fanny all alone. Rather than sleep in the house on her own, see arranged for Mr Parsons' 11-year-old daughter, to sleep with her. It is then, when they were sleeping that the eerie happenings began. During the night whilst in their slumber, they were awoken by a scratching sound emanating from behind the wooden panelling, which adorned the bedroom walls.

- Fanny was convinced that this was her dead sister warning her that was soon to die! When William Kent came back from his travels he found his lover on the brink of complete breakdown, seeing that the haunting had had such a devastating effect on Fanny, they decided to move house.

- However, that was not the end of tale, as it appears that soon after they moved, Smallpox claimed the life of Fanny.

- An argument then ensued between Parsons and Kent over the non-payment of the loan, and in an effort to deflect the debt, Parsons asserted that the 'scratchings' had since returned blamed their manifestation on Fanny's Ghost.

- In fact, Fanny had communicated through Parsons daughter through the knocking and scratchings etc., that Kent had indeed murdered his wife.
- News soon spread through London about the hauntings of 33 Cock Lane, and Parsons ever the opportunist, cashed in on the ghostly occurrences by charging the growing number of visitors' entry etc.
- However, the 'con' was soon exposed, and Parsons was sent to prison for two years.

Golden Boy of Pye Corner

- Ask most Londoners, and tourists and the majority of them will be able to tell you where the Great Fire of London started, however, ask them where it stopped and many would not have a clue.
- We have the Monument which depicts the starting point, and we have another icon for where it stopped! The Golden Boy of Pye corner, situated on the corner of Cock Lane! And Giltspur Street.

The plaque onsite tells the full story:

"The boy at Pye Corner was erected to commemorate the staying of the great fire which beginning at Pudding Lane was ascribed to the Sin of Gluttony when not attributed to the papists as on the Monument and the Boy was made prodigiously fat to enforce the moral he was originally built into the front of a public-house called The Fortune of War. Which used to occupy This site and was pulled Down in 1910 'The Fortune of War' was The chief house of call North of the River for Resurrectionists in body snatching days years ago The landlord used to show The room where on benches Round the walls the bodies Were placed labelled With the snatchers' names waiting till the Surgeons at Saint Bartholomew's could run Round and appraise them".

As we already discovered about the brothels of Cock Lane, Glitspur Street and Smithfileds, just up the road have their own place in history.

Wat Tyler famed for the Peasants Revolt in 1381, tried to stab the Mayor of London William Walworth, as the negotiations turned sour with King Richard II (who was 14 at the time) a scuffle occurred with the Mayor stabbing Wat Tyler but as he tried to getaway, he was overcome and killed by one of the King's squires.

Other famous executions also took place near here at Smithfield's one being that of William Wallace (of Braveheart fame) who was done within 1305!

Peasants Revolt Memorial at Smithfields

Route: Back to our next Pub: Head back down Giltspur St and cross over Holburn Viaduct to Old Bailey and our next pit stop The Magpie and the Stump is ahead on the right.

Before going into the pub, on your left is the Old Bailey Criminal Courts

The Old Bailey (Actually means Old Wall)

A stalwart of London's history, the courts and previously a jail have been in place for nearly a 1000 years, and the foundations of the current building are part of Roman City Wall which is over 2000 years old. Richard Whittington (f time Mayor of London, and now famous as a pantomime character who 'turned again'), became very rich in his lifetime, and when he died he bequeathed a lot of his wealth to be used to 'benefit the city'. It is believed some of this money helped build the original medieval courts. However, this was destroyed in the Great Fire of London, but was rebuilt in 1674.

The last public 'beheading' in the UK took place outside the Old Bailey prison in 1820.

Lady Justice of Old Bailey is not blind

- Made of bronze, and standing 3.7m high with her arms spanning 2.4m. She grasps in her right hand the sword of retribution, whilst in her left she holds the scales of justice (which appear equally balanced). What makes her different is she wears no blindfold.
- Lady Justice does not wear a blindfolded as her "maidenly form" is supposed to guarantee her impartiality!
- Beneath the Old Bailey is a labyrinth of tunnels from where you can still see the waters of the River Fleet.
- Hangings were so popular outside the Old Bailey that the wealthy rented 'window boxes' to watch in comfort.
- The last person to meet their demise at the Old Bailey was a George Woolfe on 6th May 1902, who apparently killed his girlfriend.
- The last woman to be publicly executed was Catherine Wilson on 20th October 1862, she was a nurse who was thought to be responsible for seven poisonings, but only after getting the people leave her their money. The sentencing judge described her as 'the greatest criminal who ever lived'.
- Standing on the site of the old Newgate Prison, if you venture around the back of Amen Court you will find the only surviving wall of Newgate Prison!

Ghost Alert:

- "This court is home to one of London's most alarming ghosts, the 'Black Dog of Newgate'. This ghost is said to be a former prisoner, who in 1596 was starving to death, along with others in London struggling from a famine. He was murdered by his cell-mates who ate him alive. It is said that he comes back in the form of a black dog to haunt the Old Bailey and used to terrorise the old prison. It is said that the court is still haunted by the black dog today…"

http://www.wegoplaces.me/haunted-places-in-london/

Magpie and the Stump

Address: 18 Old Bailey, London EC4M 7EP
Phone: 020 7248 5085
Nearest Tube: St Pauls
Hours:

Thursday	11am–12am
Friday	11am–12am
Saturday	Closed
Sunday	Closed
Monday	11am–12am
Tuesday	11am–12am
Wednesday	11am–12am

Another London pub with a very long history. It's been around for more than 500 years.

- Not unlike other pubs which strived to attract customers by providing some 'bespoke' entertainment, the Magpie and Stump was a voyeur's paradise. Grisly it may have been, but pub was ideally situated for the hangings being executed outside Newgate Prison in the 1700s. It also became known as a 'Mughouse' where people were served in the mugs they brought with them.

- To increase its reputation, and to be seen as benevolent, back then they would give a last pint to the condemned man (this practice was carried out across London at the time, where executions were carried out, we saw another example of this back on Crawl Number 1).

- The practice continued until 1868, when the public hangings were stopped. The last man to be publicly hanged here and in Great Britain, was Michael Barratt who met his demise on 26 May 1868.

- A reminder of this, and even today is used as draw to the pub, can be seen on the board outside – promoting "Last Pint Friday", it's a half-price offer 'commemorating' the pub's tradition of sending a final pint to condemned men.

-

Route: Turn into Bishops Court, and carry on down Fleet Passage then into Fleet Place. Turn right into Farringdon St, and the Hoop and Grapes pub is on your left.
Just ahead on the right before you go into the pub is Bear Alley!

Bear Alley EC4

- Bear Alley is known to have existed prior to the Great Fire of London in 1666 and in all likelihood, took its name from the Bear Inn which stood nearby. Back then the tavern names tended to reflect the pub's special draw (the Twelve Bells, the Cock Inn etc.) So as a tavern name 'The Bear' could reflect the practise of bear baiting which at the time was nigh on top of the list of popular sports.

- Tavern/Inn keepers, in an effort to promote their establishment and take custom from neighbouring pubs, were always eager to stage tournaments of one kind or another, so it is a natural assumption that bear baiting was practised here.
- In 1874 Bear Alley was turned into a cul-de-sac. And today it is a dreary place, with no real visual links back to its history.

Time for a Beer, Wine or Diet Cola!

Hoop and Grapes

Address: 47 Aldgate High St, London EC3N
1AL
Phone: 020 7481 4583
Nearest Tube: St Pauls
Hours:

Thursday	11am–11pm
Friday	11am–11pm
Saturday	8am–11pm
Sunday	Closed
Monday	11am–11pm
Tuesday	11am–11pm
Wednesday	11am–11pm

- Dating from 1721, The Hoop and Grapes has a fascinating history. Saved from demolition in the 1990s and now a grade-II listed building, this pub was the location for secret 'Fleet' weddings during the 18th century.
- Due to new statutes in 1711, which imposed fines on the wardens who were arranging weddings inside the jail pushed the 'trade' of secret weddings to outside

the prison, but still within the jurisdiction of 'Fleet rules'.

- However the Marriage Act of 1753 stopped this practice, and prospective wedding couples had to travel to Gretna Green to get married in secret, as this was the nearest place where the new Marriage Act did not hold sway!
- The original building was built in 1593 (the oldest licensed premises in the city) and was called The Castle, then the Angel & Crown, then Christopher Hills, finally becoming the Hoop & Grapes in the 1920s.
- We know it was built prior to the Great fire of London in 1666, as although the Great fire stopped, literally just around the corner, the entrance to the pub (still seen today) is timber framed.
- Now in what appears to be the first 'fire safety' legislation, following the fire, no new timber framed buildings were allowed in the city! Hence the assumption that the Hoop and Grapes is not only 'a one off' but predates The Great Fire of London.
- (Ironically the London Fire Brigade: Fire Safety computer programme is named 'Farynor, Thomas Farynor was the baker in Pudding Lane!)
- Although, through age the frame has started to sag and move, it is still secure due to some recent renovations. During these, items which 'like a modern-day time capsule' were discovered hidden in one of the bedroom walls. Items such as cattle bones, a meat cleaver and a riding whip…. I will let your imagination decide why these items would be in a bedroom!

Ghost Alert:

Built in 1721, although the cellars below probably date to before this when the River fleet was made into a canal in 1670-4. The Hoop & Grapes is built on part of the historic burial grounds of St Bride's Church which we will talk about later on in this crawl, but during its renovation there were burial remains discovered and many bodies found were moved into the British Museum. It is no surprise then that with all these bodies being discovered tales of haunting were ever present, and still persist today!

Come out of Hoop and Grapes and turn left into Stonecutter St Turn left into Shoe Lane which leads into St Brides St, and carry on in to Poppin's Court. On reaching Fleet Street, cross over and choose:
The Punch Tavern or The Old Bell; that is the question?
Before the pubs just a point to draw to your attention whilst on your route: Shoe lane:

One of the most poignant stories of the Blitz relates to the ferocious fire that swept through Shoe Lane (just off Fleet Street). Here, an AFS fireman Sidney Holder and was killed when a wall collapsed. His colleague (Rosoman) later took up painting as his form of therapy and to provide a visual memory of the horror of that night and his painting can be found at Imperial War Museum Concise Art Collection.

- In 1940 during the Second World War, London was subjected to what is now remembered as 'the Blitz' for months the Germans tried to bomb/burn the spirit and the will of Londoners. However, over Christmas there had been a lull in the bombing, but on the 29th December that came to an abrupt halt. That night the so called Second Great Fire of London began.

- Over 20000 incendiaries and 120 tons of bombs were dropped on the City. As you try to picture the scene of London aflame, try and imagine that while hell rained down from the sky some people were doing the best to put out the fires, treat the injured and survive!
- The Auxiliary Fire services were run ragged! Very little equipment, poor water supplies, low on numbers of firefighters, yet still they did more than what ever could have been expected on them. Shoe Lane is one such tale of heroism
- On that fateful night, just before 7pm the control centre sent an AFS crew to investigate reports of a fire at Shoe Lane. We now the team consisted of three people, Willian Sanson, Leonard Rosoman, and Sidney Holder, all they had for equipment was a commandeered taxi, a pump and some hose. On arrival they were met with the site of a five storey building 'well alight'.
- Unphased, the crew set to work, and for the next three hours or so they battled with the fire (remember, they were only dealing with the fire, but also having to do this while bombs dropped all around them!).
- As in common with the times people were still going about their business, (no amount of bombs was going to break their spirit!), and seeing the firefighters up against it, two passers-by, an off duty soldier and an RAF member stopped to assist them in their efforts.
- As they continued their work an AFS Officer arrived and took Rosoman away to look for more advantageous point to deploy the firehoses. As they were surveying the scene from a nearby building Rosoman recalls hearing an ominous crack, as the wall started its collapse onto the crews below.

- By pure stroke of fortune Sansom and the RAF man survived, it appears they happened to be standing right in a break in the slab of falling brickwork (maybe a window frame or the like), but Holder and the soldier were not so lucky. Although pulled from the collapse still alive, Sidney Holder died en-route to the hospital, whilst the unknown soldier died in the collapse.

Just worth a passing thought as we progress to the next pub!

On arrival at Fleet Street you can see our next watering holes. Now the dilemma!

Do we do both or just one pub, a choice only you can make. You may wish to have some food by now, to soak up all that diet cola you have been drinking.

The Punch Tavern

Address: 99 Fleet St, London EC4Y 1DE
Phone: 020 7353 6658
Nearest Tube: St Pauls
Hours:

Thursday	7:30am–12am
Friday	7:30am–12am
Saturday	11am–11pm
Sunday	11am–10pm
Monday	7:30am–11pm
Tuesday	7:30am–11pm
Wednesday	7:30am–11pm

The pub previously on this site was called the *Crown and Sugar Loaf*, but was renamed as the Punch Tavern in the 1840s, as Punch magazine had its office nearby at that end of Fleet Street.

- The first recorded appearance of Mr Punch in England was in 16 May 1662.
- Punch, the satirical magazine, was founded in 1841 at the Edinburgh Castle Tavern on the Strand, just up the road from where you are sitting. However, as the entire magazine's staff began to meet at this pub, the proprietor changed its name from the Crown and Sugar Loaf to the Punch Tavern.
- Although there has been a pub on this site since the 17th century (mentioned in Samuel Pepys diaries), it was re-fitted as a Gin Palace by the famously big spending Baker Brothers in 1893-97. It was finished just in time for Queen Victoria's Diamond Jubilee, so she would have seen it when she drove past on her way to St Paul's
- A grade II listed building, which retains a lot of Victorian artifacts, such as mirrors, wall tiles fireplaces etc. There are even some antique Punch and Judy themed paintings (painted in 1897) throughout.

The Old Bell

Address: 99 Fleet St, London EC4Y 1DE
Phone: 020 7353 6658
Nearest Tube: St Pauls
Hours:

Thursday	11am–11pm
Friday	11am–11pm
Saturday	12pm–8pm
Sunday	12pm–5pm
Monday	11am–11pm
Tuesday	11am–11pm
Wednesday	11am–11pm

- Originally built in 1670 for Sir Christopher Wren's workmen, who were rebuilding St Bride's after the Great Fire of London in 1666, the pub has changed its name numerous times over the centuries.
- Firstly, being called the Swan, it has changed its name many times over the years, once known as the Twelve Bells, (possibly as a homage to the fact that in 1800s there were only two Church's which had a 'ring of twelve bells', one was York Minster, the

other was St Brides!) and even the Golden bell before settling on its name today.

- There is a glass window which Richards and Curl admired in 1971 in their 'City Of London Pubs' book, which is still there today and gives a great feel to the interior when the sun shines through it.

- Since medieval times, Fleet Street could boast the greatest number of pubs/bars in one street and hence attracted the affectionate name of 'tippling street!' The Bell Tavern was built by Sir Christopher Wren in the 1670s for builders working on St Bride's Church, just behind the pub. It soon attracted all those working in Fleet Street's growing newspaper industry, many of whom penned out their copy while being permanently "happy"!

- Originally called the Swan, it has changed its name many times over the years, once known as the Twelve Bells, (possibly as a homage to the fact that in 1800s there were only two Church's which had a 'ring of twelve bells', one was York Minster, the other was St Brides!) and even the Golden bell before settling on its name today.

Come out of either pub and go down St Bride Lane and turn right into St Brides Avenue; Back to Fleet Street via Hanging Sword alley. Try and find the route into hanging sword alley from Salisbury Sq, if not follow Salisbury Ct to Fleet Street, turn right then enter via Hood Court.

The Church of St Bride's is justly world famous. To enter its doors is to step into 2,000 years of history, which had begun with the Romans some six centuries before the name of St Bride, daughter of an Irish prince, even emerged from legend to become associated forever with the site.

- The name St Bride's for a church off Fleet Street could not be more apt, because it plays an important role in today's wedding culture.
- While the name of St Bride comes from St Bridgit or St Bride of Kildare – a druidic slave and daughter of an Irish prince, who was born in 453. She gave away so many of her father's possessions, before following her religious calling. She is remembered by a feast day on the 1st February, when it is customary to donate to the poor.
- St Bride's as it is now, was built by Sir Christopher Wren in 1672, following the Great Fire of London, which destroyed the previous church. It is thought to be the seventh church to stand on the site since the 6th century. Samuel Pepys (1633-1703) was baptised in 1633 in the previous church on this site. Although the main church was open for worship from 1674, the tower and steeple weren't complete until 1703.
- The steeple, consisting of four tiers, each diminishing in size the higher they are, was originally 234ft high, but lost 8ft in 1764 due to a lightning strike. Back then this was the second highest church in London at 234ft only being piped to being the tallest by St Paul's Cathedral which was 366 ft tall.
- St Bride's steeple is said to have inspired the design for the modern wedding cake, However, it is believed that William Rich (1755-1812), who lived on Ludgate Hill, is responsible for the tiered wedding cake we know it today.

St Brides Church

- Living around the corner from St Bride's, he was at the time, an apprentice pastry chef, who happened to fall in love with the boss's daughter! In an attempt to impress his future father-in-law and bride to be, he sought inspiration to make a 'special' wedding cake. He found it by looking out of the window and seeing the tiered steeple of St Brides.
- Just like the traditional colour of a bride's wedding dress, the white icing was meant to symbolize purity.
- Just like the traditional colour of a bride's wedding dress, the white icing was meant to symbolize purity
- Amazingly, the steeple survived World War II, despite the actual church being fire bombed on the same night as the Shoe Lane fire on 29 December 1940.

- After the war, the church which had already been embraced by the journalists and editors of Fleet Street, financially contributed to the church's rebuilding. It was given a Grade I listing in 1950. However the damage caused by the bombing did uncover the 6th century foundations of an earlier Saxon church on the site, which can be visited on tours. Also uncovered were 'sealed coffins' in a crypt which was believed to have been closed following the Cholera outbreak in 1854.

Ghost Alert:

- "In 1650, Tom Cox, a poor coachman, was heading home down Water Lane when he saw a darkly dressed gent hailing him. Accepting one last fare for the night he picked-up the mysterious stranger who wished to be taken to St Bride's Church in London. When the coach had ratted down Fleet Street to its destination, the stranger turned to face Tom, his eyes ablaze. There in the churchyard the man transformed: growing over twice the height of any person. Matted fur burst from his skin and his teeth elongated into jagged fangs. Finally, a bear-like demon bore down on Tom Cox; who spurred by primal fear, lashed out at the creature with his whip. The beast roared diabolically, vanishing in a burst of flame". http://www.spookyisles.com/2012/07/the-bones-of-st-brides-church/

Hanging Sword Alley

Previously known as Blood Bowl Alley.

Hanging Sword Alley almost certainly got its title from a sign marking the location of a fencing and sword-fighting school. When the Whitefriars Monastery closed (following the Dissolution of the Monasteries by Henry VIII between 1536-1541), the area around here became a draw for the criminally intent, debtors etc. as it was an area with 'sanctuary' and apart from high laws, was free from normal judicial processes. Given the name Alsatia! (which was named after the ancient name for Alsace in Europe, which was itself was an area outside local legislative and juridical processes, and, therefore, it literally a place without law.) So wearing and knowing how to use a sword seemed to be a good idea if you lived or visited here. Otherwise, you were 'fair game' from any ne'er-do-well who fancied their chances to rob or maim you!

- If your thrust couldn't quite cut it in Alsatia you could easily end up skewered by one of the many vagabonds and footpads who roamed the area's maze of streets and courtyards largely untroubled by the not so long-arm of the law.
- An act of Parliament in 1697 largely removed any of the privileges formerly associated with the Whitefriars monastery, although it remained a run-down area of dubious probity.
- Of course, the unwary could get stitched up very easily when the red-top tabloids ruled the roost around Fleet Street. These days the pen is still mightier than the sword but it's wielded around Fleet Street these days by sharp-suited lawyers and financiers who moved in when the journalists and printers moved out.

Route: Back onto Fleet Street, and turn left, just down on your right you reach Ye Old Cheshire Cheese:

Fleet Street: For centuries this was the home of the newspaper industry. It ran from the Strand to the Fleet River. In times gone by it was the haunt of booksellers, writers, and printers. The first daily newspaper, the Daily Courant, was established there in 1702, and the industry grew here. Printing continued up until the 1980s when there was mass exodus.

Ye Olde Cheshire Cheese Pub

Address: 95 Fleet Street, London EC4Y 1DH
Phone: 020 7583 0216
Nearset Tube; Blackfriars
Hours:

Thursday	11am–11pm
Friday	11am–11pm
Saturday	12–8pm
Sunday	12–5pm
Monday	11am–11pm
Tuesday	11am–11pm
Wednesday	11am–11pm

- There has been a pub here since 1538, but was destroyed in the Great Fire of London in 1666 and rebuilt. Its construction contributed to its demise back then, as had it been made of stone, as with the Tipperary pub over the road, it may have survived the fire.

- However even the rebuilt version with its lack of natural light, creates an atmosphere which must replicate how it was back when it was first built and this still draws people in today.
- The small entrance, which is down a narrow side street, hides the fact that inside it is quite a large pub, made up of a multitude of little bars/room. A visit during winter will enhance your experience, as they use 'real fires' to generate warmth and this gives the patrons a certain headiness that only real flames can achieve.

Polly the Parrot:

For around 40 years, Ye Olde Cheshire Cheese was associated with an African grey parrot named Polly. The fame of the parrot was such that on its death in 1926 around 200 newspapers across the world wrote an obituary.

Brothel?

In 1962, the pub gave the Museum of London a number of sexually explicit erotic plaster of paris tiles recovered from an upper room, thought to be from the 1740s.

It's not clear why the pub was so spicily decorated upstairs. One possibility is that Ye Olde Cheshire Cheese had a little side business as a brothel going on. They could also have adorned a gentleman's club room

Ghost Alert:

- *"People they are apt of late, to condemn (most) strange things as lyes, to 'th Cheshire-Cheese you may repair, or this they will you satisfice: Having the Childrens Bones to show..." (an extract from the ballad of the Midwives Ghost. Anon),* which is a gruesome story of a tortured spectre, who in death decided to reveal whilst haunting her earthly home, and scaring the 'bejesus!' out of people who now lived there. In the 1600s society supposedly had a problem with children being killed, especially those born out of wedlock!

- The unknown author describes how the midwife Mistris Atkins had been 'murthering Babes for Parents sake'. Obviously, she saw this as some sort of civic duty! The ballad is set in Holborn in a house in Rotten Row (which was near Hyde Park). To 'prove' the ballad, it is alleged that the bones which were found can still be seen at The Cheshire Cheese pub. So you choose what to believe, maybe the children's spirits still walk this early plain where they were laid to rest! Why not check it out?

Route: Carry along Fleet Street to the Ye Old Cock Tavern;

On the way down Fleet Street you will pass The **Tipperary Pub** (you may want to pop in! but in the interest of sobriety I have chosen to just mention this pub en-route to our next stop).

The Tipperary is the oldest Irish pub in London and celebrated its 400th anniversary in 2006. Have a look at the plaque inside explaining the pub's history. The original pub dates back to 1605 and was built with stones taken from the Whitefriars Monastery, but only became an Irish pub in 1700, and was possibly the first pub outside of Ireland to serve draught Guinness. The pub was rebuilt in 19th Century, and has some fine Victorian features visible.

Before we end up in the Ye old Cock Tavern carry on down Fleet Street and turn left under the next arch into The Temple Church.

Temple Church

- The church was built by the Knights Templar, founded in the 12th century to protect pilgrims travelling to and from Jerusalem.
- The Temple Church was consecrated on the 10th February 1185.
- This was the Templars' headquarters in Great Britain.
- The Templars' churches were always built in the likeness of the Church of the Holy Sepulchre at Jerusalem, which is supposedly the site of the sepulchre where Jesus was buried.
- The Church has close links with Magna Carta. The Temple was King John's London headquarters, 1214-5. From here he issued two vital preliminary charters, and here in January 1215 the barons confronted him for the first time with the demand that he subject himself to the rule of a charter.
- It's one of just four round churches left in England.
- There are the life-size stone effigies of nine 13th-century knights lying on the floor of the Round.
- A key scene of The Da Vinci Code was set here.
- The nave, the oldest part of Temple Church, is circular, and is one of only four round churches left in England.

Okay, back to our last stop. Ye Olde Cock Tavern.

Ye Olde Cock Tavern

Address: 22 Fleet St, London EC4Y 1AA
Phone: 020 7353 8570
Nearest Tube: Blackfriars
Hours:

Thursday	11am–12am
Friday	11am–12am
Saturday	12–10pm
Sunday	12–10pm
Monday	11am–11pm
Tuesday	11am–11pm
Wednesday	11am–12am

- Ye Olde Cock Tavern dates back to 1549 and is well known for the pub with the narrowest frontage of any London pub. However the original pub was on the opposite side of the road and only moved to its current site in 1887, and is a Grade II listed building.
- Steeped in history, it was originally on the North side of Fleet Street, but has been on its existing site since

1887 and was the preferred watering hole of famous historic figures such as Samuel Pepys (apparently he arrived here by boat and was fed beer and lobster!), Charles Dickens and Doctor Johnson. Forced to close briefly in 1665 because of The Great Plague but reopened in 1668 as Ye Olde Cock Tavern and has been here since.

Ghost Alert

A floating disembodied head has been rumoured to be seen at the rear of the pub. It is reported that a barmaid whilst working in the pub in 1984 saw this head and her scream was blood curdling enough to shock customers who were sitting in the pub. After calming down, she recognised the head as belonging to Oliver Goldsmith, (Irish poet, physician and writer) whose portrait was in the pub, Oliver Goldsmith lived in the 1700s and after his death in 1774 was buried at Temple Church which is just behind the pub.

That's it for today: Our Next tour will follow London's Rich Theatre history via Pubs of course, and will start at Nell of Old Drury, Drury Lane.

Crawl Number 4
West End Theatre Land (Thespians to Spectres)

This is crawl is going to have a thespian bent to it. Having long visited various theatres in London, I already know there was a lot of history associated with the buildings and the entertainers. I will of course not be able to cover every theatre in London, as that would be impractical. You would either fall down from being too tired or being rather inebriated.

So in the words of the John Steinbeck: "*Many a trip continues long after movement in time and space has ceased*" *(Travels with Charley: In search of America).*

Pubs on Route: (Approximately 3.1 miles)

Nell of Old Drury [Theatre Royal Drury Lane] – **The Nags Head** [Royal Opera] – **The Coal Hole** [Savoy Theatre] – **The Sherlock Holmes** [Playhouse Theatre] – **The Red Lion** [Haymarket & Her Majesties Theatre] – **The Queens Head** [Criterion Theatre] – **The Dog and Duck** [Queens Theatre] – **The Argyll** [London Palladium]

Starting Point:

Nell of Old Drury:

Address: 29 Catherine St, London WC2B 5JS
Phone: 020 7836 5328
Nearest Tube: Covent Garden
Hours:

Saturday	12:30pm–12am
Sunday	Closed
Monday	5–11:30pm
Tuesday	5–11:30pm
Wednesday	12:30–2pm, 5–11:30pm
Thursday	12:30–2pm, 5–11:30pm
Friday	12:30–2pm, 5–11:30pm

One of the oldest pubs in the area and has undergone a number of changes over the years. Surprisingly there is an underground tunnel which connects the pub and the Theatre Royal (I am not sure you can still access this nowadays).

- There is a suggestion that this was used by HRH Charles II to 'cement' his illicit relationship with Nell Gwyn (during and/or after her performances) in the 1600s. (It is not clear however who used the tunnel whether it was him running to her or the other way around!)
- Supposed to have been born in a coal yard in Drury Lane, Nell seemed to have a long history with the area. When she was a teenager, Ellenore (Nell) Gwyn was taken on at the Kings Theatre (previous name of Theatre Royal) to sell oranges to the audience.
- Her 'comely' demeanour and self-confidence, let alone her physical attributes brought her to attention of the Theatre staff and was quickly taken on as an actress. She is reported to have started a series of affairs with guys called Charles, in fact Charles II (HRH) was in fact her Charles the third!
- But she obviously had an effect on Charles II (HRH) as he, when on his death bed is believed to have said to his heir, the Duke of York, "not to let poor Nellie starve", and she was 'looked after!'

Theatre Royal Drury Lane:

- This is the most recent in a line of four theatres on the same plot of land, dating back to 1663, making this London's oldest theatre. In the summer of 1665 The Great Plague hit London, and in an effort to limit public gatherings and so slow the spread, theatres and other areas of public entertainment were closed down. So on the 5th June 1665, The Theatre Royal shut its doors, and was not cleared to open again until 18 months later.

- Tragedy then hit on 25th January 1672, when a fire destroyed the theatre and a new one was designed by …guess who?… Yes you guessed it, Sir Christopher Wren and was opened in 1674.

- This incarnation of The Theatre Royal eventually degraded over time and was constantly oversubscribed, so that it was decided the only option available was to demolish it and start again, and build a bigger theatre. So, on the 4th June 1791, the theatre closed its doors for a third time.

- Opening in 1794, the new Theatre Royal Drury lane was heralded as a Fireproof Theatre, it was the first theatre to have Iron Curtains protected with integral water tanks to limit any fire spread.
- Now history has shown us that you should never make claims of indestructability! Remember the Titanic! Well some 103 years before that, and only 15 years after its opening the 'fireproof' theatre burnt down on the 24th February 1809!
- The theatre as it stands today was opened in 1812.

Ghost Alert:

Reportedly the most 'haunted theatre!' The Theatre Royal Drury Lane has been linked with many sightings and ghosts.

- ***The Man in Grey***! Arguably, the most legendary ghost is that of an 18th century dandy (complete with wig, tricorn hat and sword) who haunts the Dress Circle. He has been seen by literally dozens of cleaners over the years, and a sighting of him is usually felt to be an omen of a good run for a show. He is thought to be associated with a skeleton uncovered by workmen who were digging out a wall in a side passage in 1848. The skeleton had a dagger embedded in its ribs. Could this Dandy have fallen for an Actress, and was killed by a jealous thespian lover? Who knows but he roams the upper circle looking for something!
- ***Joseph Grimaldi:*** Joe Grimaldi was a comedian whose last benefit performance was here on 27 June 1828, and again, like the Man in Grey, is not perceived as a 'bad spirit' but is seen as a helpful spirit, whose presence seems to guide actors/actresses who may have a bit of stage fright)

rather than appear to them. "In 1948, a young American actress named Betty Jo Jones was performing badly during a run of "Oklahoma." Then, as she describes it, she felt "invisible hands" guiding her into a different position on the stage. They continued to guide her around the stage during the rest of the performance. Her performance was later described as flawless". *http://www.angelsghosts.com/drury_lane_theatre_h aunted_place_story*

- ***Charles Macklin:*** This fine fellow! Is another spectre associated with The Theatre Royal. Not being a pleasant man, Charles was constantly at odds with people and other actors in fact in 1735, Charles killed his fellow actor Thomas Hallam in an argument backstage over a wig! To win the argument and make his point, Macklin shoved his cane through the left eye of Hallam killing him instantly. Strangely, with hauntings it is normally the victim who remains on this plain as they feel they are not ready to move over to the next, however in this case it appears it is the murderer left wandering backstage, maybe seeking forgiveness.

- ***Dan Leno:*** a panto dame, who suffered from severe incontinence, and used lavender or lilac oil to hide the smell, was a well-liked actor, and performed nearly every day of his adult life, known as the Funniest man on Earth or the Kings Jester he died at the age of 42ish. Maybe it's because he died young, that he still feels the need to practice his clog dancing, or take a rest in his favourite dressing room!

- ***John Baldwin Buckstone***: Another frequent visitor from the ghostly plain John used to be an all-rounder (actor, mainly comedy, playwright and theatre manager). He seems more willing to give a guest appearance when comedies are being staged. One of today's actors (Sir Patrick Stewart; Star Trek fame,) thinks he saw an apparition when he was starring here at the theatre in 2009, in 'Waiting for Godot.' He described seeing a gentleman in a beige coat standing at the side of the stage.

https://www.theguardian.com/stage/theatreblog/200 9/aug/26/godot-patrick-stewart-ghost-theatre

- **_King Charles II:_** And of course the ghosts would not be complete without Charles II, pining for his Nell!

Route: Come out of Pub and turn right and continue up Catherine Street, and turn left at end of road into Russel Street, continue into Covent Garden and follow the square around to the right. Then turn right into James Street and walk up to where it meets Long Acre. Our next pub is in front of you.

On your way, you will walk through Covent Garden, a place steeped in history. Covent Garden gets its name due to the fact that previously, there used to be a convent/monastery located on that spot. It was dissolved with the dissolution of the monasteries by Henry VIII and the Duke of Bedford took over the land, and the name is a misspelling.

- This is a major tourist attraction known throughout the world.
- There has been some sort of market here since the 1600s.
- The Covent Garden area was home to a 'few!' brothels in the past.
- Made even more famous through films such as;

a. My Fair Lady (1964), whose main character Eliza Doolittle (Audrey Hepburn) was a Covent garden flower seller.

b. Frenzy (1972), a Hitchcock masterpiece which centres around the Covent Garden Market, and one of its fruit merchants Robert Rusk.

- Covent Garden is the only district in London to have a license for street performers and entertainers.
- The puppet duo, Punch and Judy, was first brought to the public's eye, when their appearance in Covent Garden was watched by Samuel Pepys and he recorded this event as being on 6 May 1662, this is now considered to be Punch´s birthday in the UK. There is even a Punch and Judy pub in the piazza.

Fires:

- Covent Garden Market has had two major fire fires since WWII.
  o 20 Dec 1949. Fire breaks out in cellar amongst the stored Christmas Trees.
    - Fire burns for two days and nights.
    - At end of the incident 41 firefighters were hospitalised and one officer died.
  o 11 May 1954. Fire started at about 3pm and burned well into the night.
    - 24 Fire Engines attended, tragically one Officer and two firefighters died.
    - New procedures surrounding use of breathing apparatus were implemented following these events.

Ghost Alert

Actor Bob Hoskins before making a success in films worked as a porter in Covent Garden and recalls a spooky event which happened to him there.

"I was down in the cellar at the time, when on the wall appeared a woman's face. She was wearing a nun's habit and reaching out to me with upwardly turned hands. She spoke but I couldn't tell what she said. Later I learned that Covent Garden was once called 'Convent Garden' and was owned by the Benedictines of Westminster".

http://www.mysteriousbritain.co.uk/england/greater-london/hauntings/the-nun-of-covent-garden.html

As you go around to the right of the Piazza you will come across the Royal Opera House.

- Originally known as the Covent Garden Theatre, the first theatre on this site was opened in 1732. In 1808 the theatre was destroyed by fire, reopening the following year after being rebuilt.

- However, tragedy struck yet 38 years later, when in 1856 it was raised to the ground by another fire! (for those of you following these crawls, there appears to be uneasy pattern forming with the burning down of theatres!) It was rebuilt and opened again in 1858.

- After World War II the theatre became the home for the Covent Garden Opera Company, eventually becoming the Royal Opera sometime in 1968.

- During the World War I, the theatre became a furniture repository, and in World War II it became a dance hall!

- The fire in 1856 happened when the Theatre had been let to the 'Wizard of the North' (Mr Anderson), and the end of his letting period he decided to hold a

Masked Ball, which was refused permission at first, but later it was approved by Mr Frederick Gye, who was the manager at the time. Following a night of revelry! (see over)

"At twenty minutes to five o'clock on Wednesday morning the company had dwindled down to the last dregs. Not more than two hundred persons were assembled in front of the temporary orchestra; and the musicians were closing the revels with the usual finale of God save – the Queen. At this moment a bright light was observed shining through the chinks and crevices of the flooring of the carpenters' shop overhead.

The carpenters' shop extended, with the single exception of a comparatively small space devoted to the scene painters, from one end to the other of the building, between the ornamental ceiling and the roof of the theatre. Through an open space in the floor of this atelier the central chandelier was lighted, and the place itself was generally filled with the materials of the lightest and most combustible character. The two men who had first seen the fire reached this place, but were nearly suffocated by dense black smoke, and compelled to make a speedy retreat, without having been able to open the fire mains in the floor.

Descending to the next flies they succeeded in turning on the mains, but before they could fix the hose the descending fire from the workshop above overtook them, and drove them to the next flies. The orchestra had not ceased playing the National Anthem when the sudden descent upon the stage of one of the beams around which thee canvasses are rolled gave the first intimation of danger to the motley assemblage below.

The few remaining masquers rushed precipitately to the various entrances. The flames rushed forward, and, whirling around the interior, made it at once their own. The proceeds of the night, which lay in the treasury, were rescued, as well as some valuable documents and papers from Mr Gye's private room. It was now hardly five o'clock, and yet in thee few minutes which had elapsed the doom of this noble theatre had been scaled."

http://www.fireservice.co.uk/history/theatre-royal-fire

The cause was never really nailed down, although it was determined the fire did start in the carpenter's shop, and spread rapidly, providing a spectacular night time light show. Even better than this, no one died!

Ghost Alert

The Royal Opera House, twice destroyed by fire has a long history within London. Indeed, even before being a theatre it is believed this area was a Saxon settlement known as Ludenvic which was abandoned when the Vikings decided to visit!

So with all this history, people believe ghosts must be present, it is even muted that Charlie Macklin (of Drury Lane fame) pops in now and again and causes havoc!

As you make your way to the Nags Head you will pass on your left Covent Garden tube station:

Covent Garden Tube Station:

- Shortest Tube Journey: Covent Garden to Leicester Square (260 m) and takes about 20 seconds!

Ghost Alert

- Covent Garden's tube station apparently has the spirit of William Terris causing all sorts of havoc here, even to the extent of tube staff requesting transfers.

He is a tall man in a hat, coat and gloves, and seems to be looking for revenge for his murder in 1897.

The Nags Head

Address: 10 James St, London WC2E 8BT **Phone**: 020 7836 4678
Nearest Tube: Covent Garden
Hours:

Saturday	9am–12am
Sunday	9am–11pm
Monday	9am–11pm
Tuesday	9am–11pm
Wednesday	9am–11pm
Thursday	9am–11pm
Friday	9am–12am

- Located right at the heart of London's Covent Garden, opposite the London Underground tube, The Nag's has been a McMullen pub since 1927.
- This iconic London pub is in an undeniably impressive spot where it delights tourists, locals and workers alike with true hand-crafted real ales, world beers, fine wines and hearty pub classics and after-work libations. In keeping with its cosmopolitan setting and eclectic atmosphere, we serve a hearty breakfast all day long – perfect.

P.S. Did you know that the Nag's Head was bought for the then princely sum of £7,525 Great British Pounds? God, I love the London property market!

Route: Head back down St James St, and follow the square around to your right, until you reach Southampton Street on your right-hand side. Go down Southampton St to the end of the road where it reaches the Strand. Directly opposite is our next pub, The Coal Hole.

On your way around the square you will see this Church on your right:

St Paul's Church (Actors Church)

- This Portico, was where Samuel Pepys first saw the Punch and Judy performance he wrote about in his diary (which we mentioned earlier). Often called the 'actor's church' because of its association with the theatre community.

- Situated in the heart of Covent Garden; 'The Actors Church', offers a respite from the tourist mania happening just outside its doors. Built in 1633 from a design by Indigo Jones, this 'sanctuary' and its gardens are constantly used on summer days/evenings by people relaxing and taking a break from their day to day hassle.

- The Tuscan Portico (see below) which heralds the entrance to St Pauls, maybe familiar to some as it is seen in the film of My Fair Lady.

- After its opening in 1633, Theatres also started opening up in the area, Drury Lane, Royal Opera etc., and this church soon became the local place of worship for theatre workers etc.
- Indeed, the interior walls have plaques remembering many famous actors/actresses who worshipped here, and some even had their remains laid to rest in the Church yard.

Fire at St Paul's Church

As I am sure you are appreciating as we go through these crawls, fire seems to be ever present, and constantly destroying buildings in the middle ages.

- St Paul's (Covent Garden) escaped the conflagration of the Great Fire of London in 1666, however some 130 years later it to fell fowl of the flames. During dusk, some workers who had been working on the steeple had left a pot of lead, which either spilt or boiled over causing the fire.
- Fire spread was rapid, and soon the sky became alive with dancing flames and smoke. As darkness fell, the image intensified. Within a few hours all that was left of this once grandiose building was the outside walls.
- In just three years after the fire had all but demolished St Paul's, like a phoenix rising from the flames the St Paul's that we see today was opened on August 1st 1798.
- What is just as remarkable is that at the time of the blaze, the Church was without insurance, and the cost of the rebuild was borne by the people of the parish (which included actors etc.)

As we head down towards our next stop, things start to get a bit busy information wise, but bear with it, it's all interesting!

Before we go into the Coal Hole take time to look around. On your left looking at the Pub is:

The Savoy Hotel & Theatre

- Savoy Court is one of only a few places in UK where drivers drive on right hand side of road.
- Black Taxis cabs have a turning circle of only 25 feet so they can turn around on the small roundabout in Savoy Court. (Now a legal requirement for Black Taxis).
- Grand Party: In 1905 George A. Kessler's held a "Gondola Party" where the central courtyard of the hotel was flooded in four feet of water, and an enormous Gondola house the party guests, staff all wore authentic costumes and scenery was used to create the Venice experience!
- QI moment: After an extensive refurbishment in 2007, the first guest to pull up in the hotel's custom Rolls Royce Phantom was QI presenter, Stephen Fry!

Kasper's Seafood Restaurant:

Kasper

- Named after Kasper the 2-foot-high ceramic cat which is used to ward off bad spirits. How you may ask? Well the story goes that in 1898 a diamond magnate called Woolf Joel held a dinner at The Savoy for fourteen guests.
- At the last minute one guest made their excuses and failed to attend. A diner who, must have had triskaidekaphobia (fear of 13) proclaimed that the first person to leave the unlucky table of thirteen would die soon after. Mr Joel, obviously not the suspicious type ignored this warning and went ahead with the party.
- A few weeks later he was shot dead in Johannesburg. Eager to avoid any further bad publicity, The Savoy would sit a member of staff on tables of thirteen. This was okay, but it did impinge on the ability to discuss private matters, so Kasper was born. He is now, and has been since 1927 offered to guests, where there are 13 diners to avoid anyone dying!

Savoy Theatre:

- Opened in 1881 and was the first electrically lit public building, the Hotel was an add on opening in 1889.
- In 1941 Blithe Spirit opened and ran for nearly 2000 performances, breaking records of the day.
- In 1990, Fire (AGAIN! and it's not the Middle Ages) gutted the building whilst refurbishment was being undertaken.
- The term fairy lights, comes from an operetta, Iolanthe, which opened at the Savoy on 25th November 1882. The principal Fairies had star lights in their hair, which were battery operated, and caused

a bit of a stir back then. The term has been in common use since.

On the right of the pub (as you look at it) is: Carting Lane

Carting Lane, but unceremoniously nicknamed Farting Lane!

- This is due the presence of an old gas lamp, which used work on gases, some of which came from the sewer (methane!).
- Now if you know anything about sewers, you know you do not want a buildup of methane gas, so vents were required, however the smell was not very pleasant. Cometh the hero.
- In 1895 J.E Webb, patented his 'sewer gas destructor', which vented the sewer through a street lamp where the excess gas was burned off to produce light!
- The lamp in Farting Lane is the last example of this type of lamp in London, although nowadays it runs solely on town gas.

Now on to some liquid refreshment.

The Coal Hole

Address: 91-92 Strand London WC2R 0DW
Phone: 0207 379 9883
Nearest Tube: Covent Garden
Hours:

Saturday	10am–12am
Sunday	10am–11pm
Monday	10am–11pm
Tuesday	10am–11pm
Wednesday	10am–11:30pm
Thursday	10am–11pm
Friday	10am–12am

- Why is it called the Coal hole, there is a couple of opinions, on is that it stands where the Coal cellar for the Savoy used to be, or more likely it was that it was used by the 'coalmen' who delivered coal to London via barges which came up the Thames, and was then brought up to the carters in carting lane for onward distribution, after hauling all that coal they needed a drink, and this pub was ideal.

- Inside you may find reference to the Wolf Club, which was set up by Edmund Keane, a Shakespearean Actor who felt husbands who were oppressed by their wives, and not allowed to sing in the bath, should have a place to meet!
- Formerly called The Unicorn, was established on this site in 1815.

Route: Come out of Coal Hole Pub and turn left onto the Strand, continue on down the Strand until you reach Northumberland Street on your left (just past Charing Cross Station). Turn down Northumberland Street and follow on down until you reach our next destination on the left, The Sherlock Holmes.

As you walk down the Strand, you will pass on your right the Vaudeville Theatre and the Adelphi Theatre:

Vaudeville Theatre:

The Vaudeville theatre was originally built by C J Phipps in 1870 on the site of William Robertson's failed billiards club.

The Adelphi Theatre (Lucky number 7?)

Over 200 years old, the theatre we see today is the 4th on this site and is on its 7th name!

- The Sans Pareil was built in 1806 by John Scott, a local businessman.
- In 1819 Scott sold the theatre to Jones and Rodwell who completely refurbished the theatre and staged a new opening with the name, The Adelphi.
- The second theatre built on this site in 1858 assumed the name: Theatre Royal, New Adelphi.
- The Royal Adelphi opens in 1868 with 1500 seats and 500 standing capacity. A glistening chandelier (Stroud's Patent Sun Lamp, gas powered light with cut crystal).
- In 1901 the third theatre is built on this site and opened as the Century Theatre (obviously an homage to the turn of the century!)
- However, in less than a year it went back to being the Royal Adelphi.
- The 4th theatre was built by and opening in 1930 with the same name.
- It ceased calling itself Royal in 1940, and is now the Adelphi.

The Strand:

In a book published in 1879 by Charles Dickens he describes the Strand as "one of the historical streets of London. It was formerly the water-side road, whence its name between the cities of London and Westminster. Between it and the river lay the palaces of the great nobles, and on the other side the green fields stretched away without a break to the north."

So it appears that in history, The Strand was a thoroughfare between and City and Westminster, which ran alongside the Thames, hence the term 'the Strand'.

Charing Cross railway station

- The original station was built on the site of the Hungerford Market in Jan 1864.
- It is built on a brick arched viaduct, with the height above the ground varying from 13' to 27'.
- Charing Cross Hotel opened 1865.
- A 77-foot (23 m) length original roof structure, comprising the two end bays at the south of the station, and part of the western wall collapsed at 3.45 pm on 5 December 1905.
- The part of the western wall which fell crashed through the wall and roof of the neighbouring Royal Avenue Theatre (now the Playhouse Theatre: see passage after the Sherlock Holmes Pub on this crawl) in Northumberland Avenue which was being reconstructed at the time. Six lives were lost (two workmen on the roof, a W.H. Smith bookstall vendor and three workmen on the Royal Avenue Theatre site.

Eleanor Cross

- The Eleanor Cross (built on station forecourt)__was based on the original 13th-century Whitehall Cross which was demolished in 1647.
- The original site of Whitehall Cross was used to calculate distances to and from London.
- Erected on that original site, now stands the statue of Charles I, and this is still the measuring point.

Edward I, (also known as Edward Longshanks and the Hammer of the Scots, was King of England from 1272 to 1307) erected and named these crosses after his wife. Eleanor of Castile.

She died aged 49. Longshanks was devastated, as her body was returned to London, Edward erected a Cross at each place she stopped, 12 in all, the last being at Charing Cross (Charing was a village just outside Westminster).

As you walk past the Cross, you see Northumberland Street on your left.

The Sherlock Holmes

Address: 10 Northumberland St, St James's WC2N 5D
Phone: 020 7930 2644
Nearest Tube: Embankment
Hours:

Saturday	8am–12am
Sunday	8am–11pm
Monday	8am–11pm
Tuesday	8am–11pm
Wednesday	8am–11pm
Thursday	8am–11pm
Friday	8am–12am

This pub contains a large collection of memorabilia related to the fictional detective Sherlock Holmes. Originally assembled for a display in Baker Street for Festival of Britain in 1951.

- Originally a small hotel, known initially in 1880s as the Northumberland Hotel, but changed soon after to the Northumberland Arms.

- The Northumberland Arms is mentioned in 1892 Sherlock Holmes story 'The Adventure of the Noble Bachelor'.
- The Turkish bath that Holmes and Watson used to frequent was located next to the hotel at 25 Northumberland Avenue.
- It is also proposed that by some that this pub was in fact the site of the Northumberland Hotel which appears in the iconic 'The Hound of the Baskervilles'

Some Facts About Sherlock!

- The only fictional character portrayed in more films than Sherlock Holmes is Dracula.
- Sir Arthur Conan Doyle, creator of Sherlock Holmes, was also a ship's surgeon, a boxer, Deputy Lieutenant of Surrey and a first-class cricketer who ended up in believing fairies lived at the bottom of his garden.
- Conan Doyle chose the name Sherlock in honour of Nottingham cricketers Sherwin and Shacklock. Originally it was Sherringford Holmes.
- Conan Doyle played ten first-class matches for the MCC. His batting average was 19.25 but his only wicket as a bowler was that of WG Grace.
- Holmes often said "elementary" and "My dear Watson" but never "Elementary my dear Watson."
- Sherlock Holmes Used Many Detective Techniques Before They Were *Actually* Used in the Real World!
  - Take, for instance – fingerprints. He used them in 1890 before the Scotland Yard – Britain's police force – did in 1901. He used them before the *first* recorded case using fingerprints in Argentina in 1893.

- o Holmes identified a man from his typewritten letter *years* before any official force used the technique – in 1891. The technique was first mentioned in 1894 by a guy called Hagan during his document analysis.

Place of Note:

Just down the road: at Corner of Craven St and Northumberland Avenue:

The Playhouse Theatre:

- Playhouse Theatre features a striking exterior that wraps around Northumberland Avenue into Craven Street. A grade II listed building which has a striking interior. If you go inside have a look at the lights, see what you think they look like!
- Originally the Royal Avenue Theatre, but soon afterwards dropped the Royal to become the Avenue Theatre, opened back in 1882. Mainly built and designed to stage comedies and burlesque shows but expanded to other genres as the audience numbers dictated.
- Whilst being renovated in 1905, part of Charing Cross Railway station collapsed onto the theatre killing six workers. This tragedy put back the opening of the 'Playhouse Theatre' until 1907.

- In 1951 it was taken over by the BBC and used to film live performances, such as The Goons Show and Steptoe & Son to name but two.
- In the 1960s the Beatles performed here for BBC TV shows.

Route: A little trek now, but it will be worth it!
Come out of pub and go straight down to Northumberland Ave. Turn right into this avenue and follow until you reach Trafalgar Sq. go around the square clockwise until you reach the 3rd exit, Cockspur Street. Go along this road and cross over Pall Mall into Haymarket. Go up Haymarket and take first left into Charles II Street. This then joins St James Square which you will follow around to the right, and the turn right into Duke of York Street, you next watering hole is up this street on the left. The Red Lion Pub.
On your route:

Trafalgar Square:

- The centrepiece of Trafalgar Square is Nelson's Column, which was built to honor Admiral Horatio Nelson, who led the British to Victory at the Battle of Trafalgar.
- During the battle, Nelson had 27 ships against 33 French and Spanish ships. They lost 22 ships, and the Brits lost NONE! (One trick Nelson used was to paint all our ships black and yellow to distinguish them in battle).

- Nelson's Column is 169 foot 3 inches high. Originally it was thought it was higher but in 2006 during a makeover they discovered the real height.
- The base of Nelson's Column is decorated with four bronze relief panels, each 18 feet square, which were cast from captured French guns. They depict the Battle of Cape St Vincent, the Battle of the Nile, the Battle of Copenhagen and the Death of Nelson at Trafalgar.
- Every year a Christmas tree is placed in the centre of the Square, a gift from Norway as a thank you for Britain's support during World War II.

- In respect to Norway, and their tradition, the Christmas lights are hung vertically instead of going around the tree.
- Supposedly, If Hitler had successfully taken Britain during World War II, he planned to relocate Nelson's Column to Berlin as a war spoil.
- In Trafalgar Square, in 1926, the smallest police station was created. A one-man police 'box' so officers could keep an eye on gathering crowds. Nowadays it's a cleaners' cupboard!
- The statue of Charles I upon his horse, is the site of the original Whitehall Cross from where distances, to and from London are still calculated.

On your left, as you go around the square is

Admiralty Arch: written above it are the words
ANNO: DECIMO: EDWARDI: SEPTIMI: REGIS: VICTORIÆ: REGINÆ: CIVES: GRATISSIMI: MDCCCCX: (*In the tenth year of King Edward VII, to Queen Victoria, from most grateful citizens, 1910*)

In the past the First Sea Lord lived here.

Fallacy! The nose on the inside of the Arch, purportedly a homage to the Duke of Wellington, and is touched by the Household Calvary riders as they pass! In fact it is one of the seven noses of Soho (although one is not in Soho!), which were put in by artist by Rick Buckley in a protest about all the CCTV being used. (Turning your nose up to authority?)

Locations of seven noses:
1. Admiralty Arch
2. Great Windmill Street
3. Bateman Street
4. Meard Street
5. Dean Street
6. Endell Street
7. Floral Street

Cockspur Street

Cockspur Street is so named because the spurs with which the birds were equipped to cause greater damage to the combatants were made and sold here.

Haymarket Theatre

- First Haymarket Theatre built in 1720, on site of Kings Head Inn.
- This theatre cost £1500 to build and decorate.

- Built in an area which was rife with villains, crooks, and market-traders who had laden carts with hay etc.
- 60 years after the Great Fire, London was now Europe's biggest city, where the rich and poor lived side by side.
- When it opened its doors in 1720, the 'Hay Market' attracted a lot of 'development issues! (some may say problems)'.
  - Theatres at the time required a Royal Patent or Royal Charter giving them permission to operate, Mr Potter didn't have one.
  - The Little Hay Theatre as it was known, never got the Royal Patent, and was regularly closed down for taking money on the door by the constabulary.
  - Surviving on a day to day basis, Potter put on any plays that he could, until in in 1729 a new playwright Henry Fielding joined the theatre and this injected new plays which were well attended.
  - However, in 1734, he wrote a play called the 'Historical Register for 1736' which had a character called 'Quidam' (who was a 'naughty' politician!) who was instantly recognisable as a satirical caricature on the then Prime Minister Robert Walpole.
  - He was not best pleased, consequently his retaliation was felt for the next 231 years! Walpole introduced the Licensing Act 1937, which gave the Lord Chamberlain extreme powers of censorship and these remained in place until 1968.
  - The Little Hay was forced to close for a number of years and did not get the Royal

Patent until 1767 when it re-opened as The Theatre Royal Haymarket.

Ghost Alert:

- One ghost which reputedly spends his time walking around backstage and the dressing rooms is John Baldwin Buckstone, actor/manager (14.09.1802-31.10.1897).
- Sightings have been verified by some famous thespians such as Dame Judi Dench, Donald Sinden and Patrick Stewart as well as theatre staff who have heard him rehearsing his lines.
- After having a long history with the theatre, he became engaged in 1854 to Fanny Fitzwilliam who died of cholera shortly before their wedding day. So distraught! John Buckstone eventually married Isabella Copeland, Fanny's sister (Ou err!). He died at home following several years of ill health.
- Mr Buckstone is a welcome ghost, as purportedly he only puts in an appearance when a performance is destined to make it big.
- Another former manager of the theatre, David Morris, is reported to return maybe once a decade to the theatre just to cause trouble for a single night, before returning to his grave.

Her Majesties Theatre:

- Seeing an opportunity to break the duopoly of the patent theatres, John Vanbrugh bought some stables for £2000 in 1703 in order to build a new theatre on the Haymarket.
- This would be the third theatre in the West End and provide an alternative to the Theatre Royal Drury

Lane (1663) and the Lincolns Inn (1660) later to become the Theatre Royal, Covent Garden (1728)

- These three theatres would form the design/template for future theatres.
- There have been theatres on this site since 1703, the latest finished in 1897.
- First theatre called the Queens Theatre (renamed the Kings Theatre after Queen Anne died) burned to the ground on 17th June 1789 (another one claimed by the flames!)
- Second theatre opened in 1791, keeping its name but again was destroyed by fire in 1867 taking adjacent properties with it. Its demise took less than an hour!
- 3rd theatre opened in 1869, now called Her Majesties Theatre, eventually being sold at auction in 1874, however its demise came soon after and was demolished in 1892.
- However, before being sold at auction, one of third theatres claim to fame is that it staged the first performance of Bizet's Carmen in 1872.
- The current Her Majesties Theatre had its foundation stone lain in 1896, four years after the demolition.
- 4 theatres on this site since 1703 the present was finished in 1897.

Ghost Alert

- After helping fund the rebuilding of the theatre, and eventually becoming its manager, Sir Herbert Beerbohn Tree, has himself appeared in numerous productions here. Apparently he loved it so much, he has not left!
- His favoured spot to watch the shows was in the top box, and this does appear to where he shows up on regular occasions, sometimes opening the door, and other times causing the temperature to drop in certain areas of the box.
- Although he has been seen by the entire cast of Cause Celebre, who watched him walk across the back of the auditorium in the 1970s.
- Seems quite apt then, that the first performance of 'The Phantom of the Opera' was staged here.

Moving on.

As you walk down Charles II Street you come to St James Square, just a little way from St James Palace, if you want to have look, follow on through the square and turn right onto Pall Mall. The palace is just down there on the left. (See below next item if moving onto the Palace) If you would rather carry on without seeing the palace or park, follow the road around to the right until you reach Duke of York Street on your right, and next pub is just up on your left.

St James Square:

- The history of the square is a snapshot of London in her prime: Henry Jermyn, Duke of St Albans was to build what is arguably London's finest square, and also cut the ribbon on the race for London's aristocrats to become hereditary landlords.
- Fire and plague was spurring the building craze in London's second city. When Charles II was restored to the English throne in 1660, he was determined to rule in a style completely opposed to that of his father:
- Like most aristocratic landlords of his time Jermyn was no architect, but he did have a vision for his development and laid out the square in plots which were to be leased to builders who were to build houses of 'substantial character'.
- He worked with Sir John Coell and Sir Thomas Clarges to make a plan, all overseen, in theory, by the King himself. The City, protective of its water supply and alarmed by the expansion of London, were not so keen, as Samuel Pepys recorded on September 2nd, 1663: "The building of St James's by my Lord St Albans, which is now about, and which the City stomach, I perceive, highly, but dare not oppose it."
- By 1666 St James's Square had its first resident – Sir William Stanley, who was living on the north side of the square. The rate books record him as owing a solitary pound, on which he defaulted. By 1667, Henry Jermyn was living in a house on the north-west

corner of York Street, later to become Chandos House.

- In 1676, St James's Square first appears as a separate place of residence, by which time the King's ex-mistress Mary, or 'Moll' Davis was living in the south-west corner. Elizabeth Pepys called her 'the most impertinent slut in the world', which is presumably how she came by the £1800 she paid for the property, aged 29.

St James Palace and St James Park

Some quick point so St James Palace, Marlborough Rd, London SW1A 1BS

- St James's Palace's beginnings were not all that auspicious. Henry VIII built it on land that had once held a hospital for women lepers dedicated to St James the Less and was built between 1531 and 1536, and used by Henry as an escape from court life.
- St James's Palace is built of brick, which is highly unusual for a palace. This is because Henry VIII felt that he didn't need the security that a castle provided.
- During the period of the English Commonwealth, Oliver Cromwell, the Lord Protector of the Commonwealth, took the palace over and converted it into army barracks.
- Kings George I, II and III lived at St James's, but a fire ravaged the palace in 1809, and destroyed the Kings accommodation. They were never replaced, and George III and Queen Charlotte moved to Buckingham House! Which eventually became Buckingham Palace in 1837.
- 'St James's Palace, where the royal family now resides in the winter season, stands pleasantly upon

the north side of the Park, and has several noble rooms in it, but it is an irregular building, by no means suitable to the grandeur of the British monarch, its master.

St James Park

- On 30 January 1649 King Charles I took a final walk through St James's Park. He was executed outside the Banqueting Hall on Whitehall later that day.
- The parks best known residents are the pelicans! Their ancestors were donated to King Charles II by a Russian Ambassador during a visit in 1664 (they came from Astrakhan in Southern Russia).
- The lake is very prominent now, but during WWIWWI it was drained and the space used by the Ministry of Shipping, and was not refilled until 1922.
- The Blue Bridge which spans the lake is the third bridge to do so, and todays one dates from 1957. The original, more decorative bridge was built in 1814 (this was replaced in 1825), following the end of the war with France (War of the 6th Coalition, March 1813 – May1814: Napoleonic Wars), There was also a Chinese style pagoda erected in the park. The celebrations that ensued, included a firework display which set fire the pagoda (destroying it), and killing one person.
- Birdcage Walk is so named because of King Charles II, who had a liking for exotic birds, and kept them in cages lining the road. At this time is was a private road, and only became open the public in 1828.

Back to the original Crawl.

Head back to St James Square, and cross the square until you reach Duke of York Street on the north side of the square. Your next watering hole is just up there on the left.

The Red Lion Pub

Address: Mall Galleries, 2
Duke of York St, London
SW1Y 6J
Phone: 020 7321 0782
Nearest Tube: Piccadilly
Circus
Hours:

Saturday	11:30am–11pm
Sunday	Closed
Monday	11:30am–11pm
Tuesday	11:30am–11pm
Wednesday	11:30am–11pm
Thursday	11:30am–11pm
Friday	11:30am–11pm

- A historic beer-house, The Red Lion near Piccadilly Circus remains ostensibly unchanged since the early 1900s. There's been a pub on the site since 1788 and, having survived the Blitz, the current building is a step back in time to an ornate Victorian gin palace.
- There has been a pub called The Red Lion on this site ever since 1788. The one you see today was

constructed in 1821 and, thanks to surviving the Blitz completely intact, has become one of London's rare examples of original ornate Victoriana at its finest.

- Uniquely, the pub is full of specially commissioned glasswork, with much of it thought to have been created by the renowned Walter Gibb and Sons of Blackfriars, using some of the most advanced engraving and etching techniques available at the time.

- While nobody is sure why there are so many mirrors, one theory is that they were deliberately commissioned by a local magistrate at the time in order to reduce the privacy of the pub's snugs, and therefore smiting the activity of local women of the night.

Route: On leaving the pub head north to the T junction with Jermyn St Turn right and head down Jermyn St At the junction with Regent Street turn left and go towards Piccadilly Circus. Here there is a small thoroughfare between Regent Street and Shaftsbury Avenue, Glasshouse Street. Go down Glasshouse Street and bear right into Sherwood Street. The Queens Head Pub is on your left next to the Piccadilly Theatre.

On your route:

St James Church

- This often-missed church was one of only three built by Sir Christopher Wren outside the City of London. The others were St Anne's (Soho) and St Clement Danes (Westminster), construction began in 1676.

- It only came about because London was growing at a rate, and local residents petitioned for a new parish to be established alongside St Martins in the Field. Eventually the Crown Estate granted the freehold, and Sir Christopher Wren was appointed as the architect in 1672.
- St James's was hit by bombs during the first phase of the London Blitz, at 7.54pm 14 October 1940.
- When the smoke cleared the next day, St James's was a burnt-out ruin, open to the elements. It remained roofless for nearly seven years.

Jermyn Street Theatre

Opened in 1994, this basement theatre is small, compact and comfortable. Sits up to 80 people and its mission statement is to 'provide talented new actors, directors and writers with the opportunity to be recognised and given a platform in smart, comfortable surroundings, and with other members of the profession'.

Worth a visit, to catch a show if you can another time:

Piccadilly Circus

- The name Piccadilly Circus could have come from a local business man. In 1612 Robert Baker, who made his fortune selling Picadils (stiff collars) built a mansion just to the north of what is now Piccadilly Circus. However the locals felt less than enamoured with it and nicknamed it Picadil Hall, and Piccadilly is a natural progression of this.
- The Statue of Eros isn't actually a Statue of Eros. As mentioned, the Earl of Shaftesbury was more of a humanitarian than a lothario so in that context it may not surprise you to know that the statue represents

Anteros, the god of selfless and mature love, not his twin brother Eros, the god of frivolous and romantic love. It was the first London statue to be cast in aluminium. It was removed during WWII to protect it from the German bombing raids.

- The bright lights of Piccadilly were shut down during WWII, but have only been switched off twice since then. Firstly for the funeral of Winston Churchill in 1965, then again for Diana, Princess of Wales in 1997
- Before being Piccadilly, this street was called Portugal Street, named after the home of after Charles II's wife Catherine of Braganza's. But it had changed by the mid-1700s
- The word 'Circus' comes from the Latin, (circular line or ring), and as so adopted by to tag on the end of Piccadilly.
- What is unusual about The Piccadilly Circus underground station is that it has entrances on every corner and is one of only a few stations with all of its premises completely underground.

The Queens Head Public House

Address: 15 Denman St, London W1D 7HN
Phone: 020 7437 1540
Nearest Tube: Piccadilly Circus
Hours:

Saturday	11am–12am
Sunday	12–10:30pm
Monday	11am–11:30pm
Tuesday	11am–11:30pm
Wednesday	11am–11:30pm
Thursday	11am–11:30pm
Friday	11am–12am

- Original pub dates back to 1736.
- In the 1850s that it was formerly used as a venue for dog and rat fighting.
- The British government banned most animal fighting at this time but it was still legal to kill rats. The Queen's Head was one of them. Every Tuesday

evening, men (women weren't allowed) would bring their dogs down to the pub where they were weighed before bets were placed on how many rats each dog would be able to kill.

- A notorious bull and terrier called Billy is reputed to of killed 100 rats in 5:30 minutes – that's one every 3.3 seconds!
- When rat baiting was eradicated towards the end of the century, the pub reinvented itself as a meeting place for pedigree dog owners. Interestingly, this meeting place to exhibit dogs soon evolved into the society that founded Crufts.

Route: Coming out of the pub, go back to Sherwood Street and turn right following it past Golden Square to the junction of Beak street, turn left then immediately turn right into Carnaby Street, follow this thoroughfare until the T junction with Great Marlborough Street, then turn left and first right into Argyll Street. The Argyll Arms is up on your left.

On your route:

Golden Square

- Believed to have been laid down by Sir Christopher Wren around 1670.
- The statue of George II sculpted by John Nost in 1724 came from Cannons House in March 1753.
- There is confusion about whether the statue represents King George II of Great Britain, or King Charles II, as noted on the signage in Golden Square. Folklore states that the statue was accidentally won at auction, when the winning bidder raised his hand

to greet a friend. The amount of money he paid was so low that he decided not to contest and gave the statue as a gift to the people of Golden Square.

- William Pitt the Elder was born in the Square in 1708.

Carnaby Street

- The area around Carnaby Street during the Great Plague (1665-6) was used as a mass burial.
- After the Great Fire of London in 1666, it became residential; Karnaby house was built in 1683, giving the street its name.
- The title "The King of Carnaby Street" was bestowed on John Stephen, as he opened the first boutique "His Clothes", in 1958 which then set the trend.
- The opening of Lady Jane boutique on Carnaby Street in May 1966 involved live models dressing and undressing in the window of the shop. Henry Moss, the owner of the boutique was arrested and fined £2 for obstructing the highway, due to the large crowd of men who had gathered to watch the spectacle.
- The Kinks hit, Dedicated Follower of Fashion, (1966) even references Carnaby Street: "Everywhere the Carnabetian Army marches on, each one a Dedicated Follower of Fashion". Which is testimony to how this street was perceived at the time.
- Even the Americans recognise the importance of this street, in a Simpsons episode, Bart and Lisa appear on Carnaby Street wearing Mod fashions.
- In trying to draw attention to the opening of a new shop 'Tom Cat', Tom Jones walked down the street with Christine Spooner (who was a casino patron, in the bond film Casino Royale from 1966) and a live cheetah on a lead.

Hamleys

- Consisting of seven floors, each of which dedicated to different types of toys. Stocked with over 450,000 different toys.
- In business for over 255 years, it was awarded a Westminster City Council Green Plaque in 2010, dedicated to William Hamley.
- Hamleys has been granted Royal Warrants twice. Once in 1938 by Queen Mary, and another in 1955 by Queen Elizabeth II.
- Hamleys, although being hit by German bombs during the London Blitz, the store remained open for business. Staff was resolute, they wore tin hats and served the customers from the front door, rushing in to get the toys.
- Hamleys is the oldest toy shop in the world. Formed as "Noah's Ark" in 1760 by William Hamley in High Holborn and carried everything from rag dolls to tin soldiers.
- Relocated to Regents Park 1881.
- Original store was destroyed by fire in 1901.
- Hamleys has a pair of mascots, giant bears named Hamley and Hattie.

London Palladium

- The London Palladium opened on Boxing Day 1910 with the first 'grand variety bill' featuring acts as diverse as Nellie Wallace and classical actor Martin Harvey. The Frank Matcham designed building occupies a site which was previously home to a Corinthian Bazaar, Hengler's Grand Cirque and the National Ice Skating Palace.

- The Palladium hosted its first *Royal Variety Performance* in 1930 and the following year the first Crazy Week which brought together the famous Crazy Gang.
- In 1940 *Top of the World* played only four performances before being closed by the Blitz but the theatre soon reopened in 1941 with Max Miller and Vera Lynn in *Apple Sauce.*

Ghost Alert:

- The theatre stands on the site of the residence of the Duke of Argyll, and the Crimson staircase at the back of the Royal Circle is believed to be a remnant of that house, and it's here a lady has been seen on numerous occasions, by staff and actors alike.
- One witness, Arthur Cow, had actually seen the figure of 'a beautiful lady in a marvellous crinoline dress' when, 'doing a bit of cleaning up behind the Royal Circle'. This lady is allegedly to be the ghost of Helen Campbell, a former resident of Argyll House.

Argyll Street

- Little known fact by the masses, a Major-General William Roy designed and created the roots which went on to become the Ordnance Survey Maps we know today, and he lived here on Argyll Street.
- Set up the year after Roy died, the Board of Ordnance produced its first map of Kent in 1801, and covered the rest of Great Britain over the following sixty years.

On to our next stop, as you must be getting thirsty by now!

The Argyll Arms

Address: 18 Argyll St, London
W1F 7TP
Phone: 020 7734 6117
Nearest Tube: Oxford Circus
Hours:

Saturday	10am–12am
Sunday	10am–11pm
Monday	10am–11:30pm
Tuesday	10am–11:30pm
Wednesday	10am–11:30pm
Thursday	10am–11:30pm
Friday	10am–12am

First Licensed in 1741, and now a Grade II listed pub is named after the second Duke of Argyll, who lived in a mansion where the Palladium now stands.

Rumour has it that a secret tunnel once connected the pub to the duke's mansion. (I can find no evidence of this, but may be similar to the one at Nell of Old Drury.) The pub you see today provides a fascinating social and historical narrative thanks to its Victorian 'snug' areas built to separate the social classes.

https://www.nicholsonspubs.co.uk/restaurants/london/thearg
yllarmsoxfordcircuslondon

That concludes another crawl. I hope you have enjoyed this one, and I leave you with this passing thought:

"Always do sober what you said you'd do drunk. That will teach you to keep your mouth shut."

~ Ernest Hemingway

Crawl Number 5
Mayfair (Rags to Riches)

Check opening times as some of these pubs are closed at weekends!

Right, this crawl leads us through what most people (and the Monopoly board) feel are the more expensive/highfalutin areas of London. But history may have something else to say!

Grown from the site of an annual fair in the late 1600s to the splendour we see today, this area has tales of drunken debauchery, ghosts, prostitution and political scandal all of which we shall touch on during our own libation laden crawl.

The editor of the Observator at that time recounts of the 'fair', "*Oh! The piety of some people about the Queen, who can suffer things of this nature to go undiscovered to her Majesty, and consequently unpunished! Can any rational men imagine that her Majesty would permit so much lewdness as is committed at May Fair, for so many days together, so near to her royal palace, if she knew anything of the matter? I don't believe the patent for that fair allows the patentees the liberty of setting up the devil's shops and exposing his merchandise for sale.*"

So onward!

"In wine there is wisdom, in beer there is Freedom, in water there is bacteria."

~ Benjamin Franklin

Pubs on Route: (Approximately 2.01 miles)

The Goat Tavern – Burlington Arms – Masons Arms – The Running Horse – Audley – The Punchbowl – Ye Grapes – The Rose and Crown

Starting Point:

The Goat Tavern

Address: 3 Stafford St, Mayfair, London
W1S 4RP
Phone: 020 7629 0966
Nearest Tube: Green Park
Hours:

Sunday	12–10:30pm
Monday	11:30am–11pm
Tuesday	11:30am–11pm
Wednesday	11:30am–11pm
Thursday	11:30am–11pm
Friday	11:30am–11pm
Saturday	12–10:30pm

The pub name is possibly linked in some way with The Worshipful Company of Cordwainers whose coat of arms show three Goat heads, this is one of the Livery Companies of the City of London. Cordwainers were workers in fine leather, and are so named after 'Cordovan' the fine white leather produced from goatskin, and originated in Spain (Cordova).

Previously all fine leather makers, were originally classified under this title; however, this has been superseded today by just being linked to fine leather footwear, including boots.

- This pub has a history dating back to 1686.
- Built on the site of Clarendon House which stood here from the 1660s to the 1680s, and was deemed to be the grandest private residence in London at the time.
- Finished in 1667 at a cost of over £38,000 the home was shrouded with controversy from the start.
- Allegations were made that its owner Edward Hyde (1st Earl of Clarendon), had 'got hold of' stone that was earmarked for the repairs to St Paul's Cathedral following the Great Fire.
- This was partially why he fell from King Charles II's grace, and so fled to France where he eventually died.
- Eventually the site was sold and the following streets were built Dover Street, Albemarle Street, and Bond Street.
- In 1697, The Goat Tavern was owned by William Underwood who, sold the remainder of his 52-year lease to Robert Munden.
- It then become the property of a Vicar for a few years before being sold one and rebuilt in 1878.

Route: Turn left out of the pub onto Stafford Street, at the T junction with Old Bond Street turn left and then take the first right into Burlington Gardens. Continue along this road then take your second left and Old Burlington Street. The Burlington Arms is at the end of this street on your left.

On your route you will pass the rear entrance to;

Burlington Arcade!

Interesting facts about the Arcade:

- It has the Oldest and smallest Police force in the world (The Beadles).
- Since 1819 patrolled by the Burlington Beadles who uphold a strict code of conduct dating from Regency times.
- Originally recruited from Lord Cavendish's regiment The Royal Hussars, they are easily identifiable with their Victorian styled frock coats, and gold buttons etc.
- Many of the shopkeepers lived either above or below their shops and in the early days, the upper level of the arcade had quite a reputation for prostitution.
- To avoid being caught 'plying their wares!' prostitutes were warned by their pimps of the approaching Beadles by bursting into song or whistling!
- Whistling was also used by the 'Toms' (slang term for prostitutes, which one possible evolution of this term being linked to cockney rhyming slang, Thomas More = Whore, and another linking it to prostitutes from the Mayfair area) who worked the upper levels to warn the pickpockets that the 'Beadles were about'
- Even today, the rule of not singing and whistling are still banned in the arcade and rigorously enforced by the Beadles.
- Other rules include, not being allowed to 'hum' 'hurry' or 'behaving boisterously!'
- In 1964 a Jaguar Mark X drove down the arcade and provided the getaway car for a jewellery heist, the perpetrators of which were never caught.

- Since then bollards have been installed at the entrances to stop this happening again.

Also, if you detour and follow Old Bond Street and carry on into New Bond Street then turn right into Clifford Street, and Old Burlington Street is on your left, you will pass a very unusual sculpture: This is called 'Allies' and depicts Churchill and Truman sitting on a bench.

This bench was designed by Lawrence Holofcener. It is known as 'Allies', and was given by the Bond Street Association to commemorate 50 years of peace.

Ghost Alert:

- Since the early fifties a poltergeist named Percy has be believed to be the cause of things being moved about, in the late 70s when the shops (a leather goods shop and a tobacconist) had been closed overnight. Things were removed from the shelves and rearranged on the floor, in a circle or semi-circle, with no sign of forced entry!

- This happened over a four-month period and has not occurred since…. Well not yet!

The Burlington Arms

Address: 21 Old Burlington St, London W1S 2JL
Phone: 020 7479 7620
Nearest Tube: Piccadilly Circus
Hours:

Monday	12–11pm
Tuesday	12–11pm
Wednesday	12–11pm
Thursday	12–11pm
Friday	12pm–12am
Saturday	12pm–12am
Sunday	Closed

The pub was founded in 1720 as the Coach & Horses. It was rebuilt in 1782 and may have become the Burlington Arms at that time, but the present public house was rebuilt in 1882 by George Treacher.

Tucked away in a little side street this pub is in a very salubrious area of London, and just down the road from New Bond Street and Burlington Arcade.

Route: Turn right out of pub into Boyle Street then first left into Saville Row, follow straight on into Mill Street, then continue to the junction with Maddox Street. Your first stop The Masons Arms is opposite you now.

On your route:

Savile Row

- Originally named Savile Street, built between 1731 & 1735 as part of the development of the Burlington Estate.
- Initially, the street was occupied by military families, along with some politicians. Some well-known people have also resided here, such as William Pit the Younger, Richard Sheridan, and Jules Verne had his eccentric character Phileas Fogg residing at 7 Savile Row (see below).
- Tailors began to move in and around Savile Row in the late 1700s, then by 1803 into Savile Row itself
- In 1846, Henry Poole, designer of the original dinner jacket/tuxedo expanded his family owned business, which was in Old Burlington Street by creating an entrance at 37 Savile Row. Even then the address 'Savile Row' conjured up images of professional tailors.
- As tailoring took hold, the building designs were altered to allow more light in etc. and only No. 14 still retains much of the original external features.

- On 30 January 1969 at 3 Savile Row, The Beatles surprised the central London district with an impromptu roof top concert.

Incidents of Note:

During the blitz of the Second World War, Savile Row had two major incidents.

- September 16: high explosive bomb completely demolishes the house at No.7 (luckily Phileas Fogg was not home ☺), causing damage to surrounding properties, and a major Coal Gas leak, it was felt so serious at the time, no smoking signs were put up!
- September 24: eight days later, 21a was set alight by incendiary bombs. Followed by a direct hit, again surround properties were damaged, even the recently opened Police Station.
- The first parachute bomb to fall in Westminster fell on the corner with Boyle Street, again causing damage to the police station and starting many fire which had to be dealt with by the AFS.
- 3 policemen died during these events.

The Masons Arms

Address: Maddox St, Mayfair W1S
1PY
Phone: 020 7491 7809
Nearest Tube: Oxford Circus
Hours:

Monday	11am–11pm
Tuesday	11am–11pm
Wednesday	11am–11pm
Thursday	11am–11pm
Friday	11am–11pm
Saturday	11am–12am
Sunday	Closed

The first records showing this property was as a Tailors in the 1800s it later was sold and changed its usage to a hairdressers, and finally changed into the pub we see today in 1848, and was called the Masons Arms as a testament to the stonemasons working in the area at the time. There are also historical ties to the freemasons. Although the area was heavily bombed during WWII the Mason arms remained intact.

Local residents have included Sir John Herschel (Astronomer) and Charles Babbage who invented the computer, but there are no Blue Plaques on this road for them

Also on Maddox Street: The Beatles and Rolling Stones had offices here during their heydays!

Route: Come out of the pub and turn right down Maddox Street. Turn right into Avery Row, continue down until junction with Brook Street, cross over into South Molton Lane. Then take the first left into Davis Mews and continue to the end of the road, and the Running Horse is on your right.

On your route down Maddox Street you will cross over New Bond Street!

- Now strange but true. On the original London Monopoly Board you may remember a street call Bond Street which cost £320, a challenge! Try and find Bond Street on a map of Mayfair today, there is Old Bond Street, New Bond Street but no Bond Street (there is however a tube station!)
- In 2015, an updated board was created using up to date house prices, look what's the most expensive!

The Running Horse

Address: 50 Davies St, Mayfair, London W1K 5JE
Phone: 020 7493 1275
Nearest Tube: Bond Street
Hours:

Friday	7:30am–12am
Saturday	10am–12am
Sunday	Closed
Monday	7:30am-12am
Tuesday	7:30am–12am
Wednesday	7:30am–12am
Thursday	7:30am–12am

A tavern since 1738, with a neat upstairs dining room for traditional European cuisine.

Established in 1738, The Running Horse is the oldest public house and kitchen in Mayfair.

Mark Twain once said a mine is a hole in the ground which is owned by a liar. The locals here have heard that before to, but their version is that he talked too much and backed the wrong holes!

This pub seems to have been adopted as the unofficial meeting spot for the mining industry. Used as a pressure release for local people involved in the mining industry, and many a 'deal' has been sealed here.

Try the Whip cocktail bar upstairs!

Route: Come out of pub and head down Davis Street until you reach Mount Street on your right. Go along Mount Street until your reach your next pub 'Audley' on your right.

On your route prior to turning into Mount Street, ahead of you on your left is Berkeley Square, and there are a few interesting titbits which you may be interested in.

Song: A Nightingale Sang in Berkeley Square;

- The song was written by Manning Sherwin, Eric Maschwitz in a small French fishing village 'Le Lavandou' nowadays a holiday and second home destination for many Brits.
- Written prior to the start of WWII, apparently the title was 'borrowed' from a story by the same name, authored by Michael Arlen.
- The song had its first performance in the summer of 1939 in a local bar, where the melody was played on piano by Manning Sherwin with the help of the resident saxophonist. Maschwitz sang the words while holding/sipping a glass of wine.
- It was soon to become a song which was sung throughout the war, and indeed conjured up happier times, when lovers could stroll hand in hand, and hear the sounds of birds singing, rather than the sounds and sights of war. A song for hope! Add the fact that

is was sung by the forces sweetheart, Dame Vera Lynn, it was destined to become legendary.

Enough sentiment for the time being:

Ghost Alert:

There is not one but two famous haunted houses located in Berkeley Square! At number 44 resides the ghost of Lady Isabella Finch's servant, and at number 50 this is reputedly. ***London's Most Haunted House***.

44 Berkley Square

- It was designed and built in 1742 by William Kent, and was to be the new residence of Lady Isabella Finch.
- She was the Maid of Honour to Princess Amelia who was sister the then regent George II. Parties and Soirees abounded for the great and the good of the time.
- All of this frivolity took place under the supervisory eye of the Princess's devoted major-demo (head of the household) whose bearing was emphasised by his demeanour, green livery and a very nice powdered wig!
- For over 200 years, for whatever reason the major-demo has chosen not to pass over the ethereal plane, and continues to been seen supervising the goings on from the staircase.
- Albeit his visits appear to be but a brief encounter he still seems intent on ensuring there is 'no funny business' going on, and once satisfied simply drifts through the building to his old bedroom at the top of the house.

50 Berkley Square (I will spend a little time on this one as it deserves it!)

- Never judge a book by its cover! An unconvincing façade, this Georgian building does not look terrifying at all!
- Even the interior is one of splendour, mirrors and marble floors etc. Nothing like the image of a haunted dungeon, so what should the most haunted house look like, well not like this!
- The image of horror/terror is one which has been planted in our minds by old Hammer Films and Hollywood but this is reality…. or is it?
- How did it get the title then of the Most Haunted House in London?
- Charles Harper in *Haunted Houses*, published in 1907 stated that "… It seems that a Something or Other, very terrible indeed, haunts or did haunt a particular room. This unnamed Raw Head and Bloody Bones, or whatever it is, has been sufficiently awful to have caused the death, in convulsions, of at least two foolhardy persons who have dared to sleep in that chamber…"
- The first fatality was a 'brave' nobleman who took great pleasure in dismissing the stories of the hauntings, and was happy to stake his reputation on the fact that it was all some mischievous prank by spending the night.
- In an effort to ensure his safety, a plan was set in place, whereby if he felt unwell or required some help he would simply 'ring' the servants bell and his friends would come running.
- Just after midnight a feint ringing was heard, this was quickly followed by the rapid ringing of the servant's bell.

- True to their word, his friends rushed to his aid, only to be confronted by their friend lying prostrate on the floor, struck dumb and his face distorted through fear. His eyes were swollen to the point of leaving their sockets. The shock being too much he soon died.
- News spread quickly throughout London, and no one was brave enough to take up the lease on the property, and so it remained empty of 'human life'.
- Passers-by still heard and saw strange things, which further endorsed its growing reputation.
- However, the house was not yet done! One dark and windy night, two sailors on shore leave in London needed a place for the night and stumbled upon the 'empty' house!
- Seizing the opportunity, they broke in and for some unknown reason (maybe they were drawn to it) chose to sleep in the haunted room.
- Whilst in their slumber they suddenly woken by the sound of someone coming up the stairs.
- Just then the door burst open and they were confronted by some shape, mass, who knows what, but it was enough to strike fear in their hearts. One managed to rush past it and escape the house only returning when accompanied by a local 'bobby'.
- On his return, he saw his friend's body draped over the spiked railings at the front of the property, obviously he felt his chances of survival were better jumping from the window rather than face the spectre!

What has caused the haunting?

- Looking back at Charles Harper *Haunted Houses,* he believed that the house had once belonged to a Mr Du Pre of Wilton Park. This kind gent decided to lock his lunatic brother in one of the upper rooms. So disturbed was his brother he remained under lock and key and was only fed remotely. No one had contact with him. When he eventually died, his soul remained behind to haunt anyone who dared enter his prison!

- Other theories include a jilted lover and his nocturnal ramblings, but whatever the reason or the cause it is apparent that there is something strange about this address.
- And it's not an ancient story, as recent as 2001 issues have been reported …. are you feeling brave?

On to the next watering hole:

The Audley

Address: 41 to, 43 Mount St, Mayfair
W1K 2RX
Phone: 020 7499 1843
Nearest Tube: Bond Street
Hours:

Monday	11am–11pm
Tuesday	11am–11pm
Wednesday	11am–11pm
Thursday	11am–11pm
Friday	11am–11pm
Saturday	12–10:30pm
Sunday	12–10:30pm

Stemming from the late Victorian Era, this pub seems to have joined the 21st Century whilst maintaining the charm and grandeur of its rebirth in 1889.

Originally established in 1730 as The Bricklayers Arms and was given a makeover in 1888 following a directive from the Duke of Westminster Hugh Grosvenor. He allowed the landlord to retain the license on the condition that the name was changed to 'Audley Hotel'.

The architect was Thomas Verity, who had previously worked on other London landmarks such as assisting in the erection of the South Kensington Museum and The Royal Albert Hall. In 1870 he won an open competition to build the Criterion Theatre. A lot of his original design can still be seen today at the Audley, check out the Clock situated in the main bar, and the original crystal chandeliers, which add to the 'Olde-Worlde' lustre.

Route: Turn Right into Molton St and stay on this road until you reach the junction with Park lane. Turn left down Park Lane and then take second left on South Street. A little bit of a walk now down South Street until it joins Farm Street and your pub is just on the left, The PunchBowl.

On your route:

Now things take a turn as we are faced with Park Lane, Marble Arch to your right and Hyde Park opposite as you enter Park Lane.

Let's Start with Marble Arch

- Marble Arch was designed in 1928 by J Nash, to commemorate the British victories at Trafalgar and Waterloo. The three arches represent England, Scotland and Ireland.
- It was originally designed to include sculptures that depicted the victories of British forces during the Napoleonic Wars.
- The Marble Arch itself is made of Carrara marble.
- In 1571, the Tyburn Tree was near the site of the Arch. The 'Tree' or 'Triple Tree' was a form of

gallows where several convicted souls could be hanged in tandem, thus saving time!

- The hangings at Tyburn and other hanging sites, (as discussed in earlier chapters) gave rise to the popular phrase "one for the road" which refers to the practice of allowing a condemned man to have one last drink at any ale house on their way to their death!

- Transported to the gallows by wagon, it was policy for one of the guards minding the prisoner to remain in charge of the cart. (Much akin to todays 'nominated driver!' So as they weren't allowed to drink, thus the saying "on the wagon" came into being.

- Historically, only a few chosen people have been allowed to process through the arch, and these included the Royal Family and the Royal Horse Artillery.

- Marble Arch was originally the entrance to Buckingham Palace, but was moved to Hyde Park when Queen Victoria expanded the palace.

- There is also a small police station within the structure, not used nowadays though!

Hyde Park:

- Hyde Park is a big place: 625 acres in total.
- The Park once belonged to monks, however when King Henry VIII founded the Church of England, he brought about the dissolution of the catholic monasteries (1536-1541), which is also sometimes known as the suppression of the monasteries, and once that happened he took over the land. Not renowned for his known for his magnanimity Henry

decided to keep the whole park for himself using it as a personal hunting ground.

- King Charles I however was a different Regent, and he decreed the park should be open to the public (1637) and since then it has never closed.
- Speakers Corner was established after 1872, when following a rather violent protest which involved the Police being called in to calm matters down, the authorities really 'thought out of the box'. Rather than react in knee jerk manner, they decided to provide a platform whereby people could express their views on anything, so long as they did not incite violence.
- The Serpentine, a man-made lake built between 1827-1831 as a memorial for Queen Caroline hated wife of George IV. (see below) There's also a tradition in which a few hardy Londoners take a dip in the Serpentine every year on Christmas morning.
- The main entrance to the park is known as Apsley Gate was erected from the designs of Decimus Burton in 1824–25.
- An unusual piece of nature exists in the park and that is the Weeping Beech, *Fagus sylvatica pendula*, aka, "the upside-down tree".

The PunchBowl

Address: 41 Farm St, London W1J 5RP
Phone: 020 7493 6841
Nearest Tube: Green Park
Hours:

Monday	12–11pm
Tuesday	12–11pm
Wednesday	12–11pm
Thursday	12–11pm
Friday	12–11pm
Saturday	12–11pm
Sunday	12–10:30pm

Dating from *circa* 1750. It is the second oldest pub in Mayfair, and is a Grade II listed building by English Heritage. It is a Georgian building and, although altered over the years, retains many period features including a dog-leg staircase, internal cornicing and dado panelling.

Guy Ritchie (British Film maker) has called time on his career as a pub landlord. He has sold his part ownership of the

PunchBowl after five years. When he bought the 250-year-old pub, it became a haunt of the rich and famous.

Route: Leave pub and go forward in to Chesterfield Hill, and follow it down until you get to the third on the left Charles Street. Turn down here and follow down until you see Hays Mews on your left, and your next pub is right in front of you.

On your route

As you enter Charles Street and before you turn left, look to your right and you may just see Chesterfield Street. Have you ever heard of Beau Brummell? Well!

- Beau Brummell was famous not only for his elegance in dress, but also for his wit.
- He was a famous figure in the higher echelons of Regency England, and a friend of the Prince Regent, the future King George IV.
- His life was a rollercoaster, after his military career where he made friends with the Prince; he continued to move in the upper circles of society, but without the financial clout.
- He moved to Chesterfield Street where he became a 'dandy'. Due to his ways and humour he was liked and accommodated, and although he managed to steer away from the financial expense of the 'high society' betting antics he did not scrimp on his clothes.
- Eventually it all caught up with him, and in 1816 he fled to France, where he eventually died, to escape 'debtors prison'.
- 'Charles Street occupies part of the lawns of Old Berkeley House, which was the mansion which was

225

owned by the cavalier Lord Berkeley of Stratton, who during the civil war between Charles I and Parliament, distinguished himself as the 'hero of the Stratton fight'.

- Soon after the Restoration of the Monarchy in 1660, Lord Berkeley was rewarded by Charles II for his loyalty to the Crown with and extensive parcel of land to the north of Piccadilly on which he constructed for himself a great house. The land was afterwards developed by his widow.

- This street, which first appears in the rate-books in the 1740s, was named after Charles, Lord Falmouth, Lord Berkeley's brother. For two hundred years until the outbreak of the Second World War these houses in Charles Street were 'the abode of rank and fashion.'

https://www.chesterfieldmayfair.com/about/history

Onto the Footman Pub, a strange history concerning the name.

The Footman

Address: 50 Davies St, London W1K 5JE
Phone: 020 7493 1275
Nearest Tube: Green Park
Hours:

Monday	7:30am–12am
Tuesday	7:30am–12am
Wednesday	7:30am–12am
Thursday	7:30am–12am
Friday	7:30am–12am
Saturday	10am–12am
Sunday	Closed

Built circa 1749 and previously called 'The Only Running Footman', there still remains evidence of the last vestiges of the unique event of Georgian competitive running with a tentative link to the cabbies of their day, let me explain!

- Frequented by the local 'footman', as this term of service started to dwindle, one went on to buy the establishment and name it after himself.

- The footman's job in the 17th century was to clear a safe passage for his master's coach, and pay any tolls ahead of the coach's arrival.
- Always looking for something to bet on, and be seen to be the 'best', the aristocracy saw an opportunity to 'race' their footmen and pitch them against other households.
- On the 3rd July 1663 Samuel Pepys recorded in his diary:
- "The town talk this day is of nothing but the great foot-race run this day on Banstead Downs, between Lee, the Duke of Richmond's footman, and a tyler, a famous runner. And Lee hath beat him; though the King and Duke of York and all men almost did bet three or four to one upon the tyler's head."
- Following the Great Fire of London in 1666 a change in the topography took place as roads/streets became less cluttered, and the need for the footman to run ahead became less important.
- As one door shut another opened, so their role evolved. A good heeled footman in 1750 could expect to earn the equivalent of £60,000 in today's money.
- Apart from working in the house, they soon became used for delivering message and letters, as they were a trusted household member.
- Tall and fit, it was not unheard of that their 'company' was sought by many women above their station!

Route: Turn left out of pub and take the first right Fitzmaurice Place, follow this all the way around to the right where it becomes Curzon St Stay on Curzon St Turn

left down an alley just after Half Moon St which leads into Shepherd Market. Ye Grapes is just down on the left.

On your route:

Curzon Street

- The village-like aura which has existed here, still survives today, and in the 1970s, it was again thrust into the limelight when just around the corner at Flat 12, 9 Curzon Place, Cass Elliot (Mama Cass) of The Mamas and Papas died on 29 July 1974 of a heart attack.
- In 1978 the same flat hit the news again when Keith Moon (The Who's drummer) rented the flat but the story goes, *"The landlord, Harry Nilson, was reluctant to rent the place to Moon, because he thought it haunted. That idea met with a comment from Pete Townshend, lead guitarist of* The Who, *that **"lightning wouldn't strike the same place twice."** Not only did he die in the exact flat, Moon was the same age, 32, as Elliott when she died there four years earlier."*
  http://www.mysteryinthehistory.com/mysterious-deaths-musical-history/
- Starting life simply as 'Mayfair Row', Curzon Street is now one of Mayfair's most famous addresses.
- Curzon Street has also been immortalised in literature and has seen a wide range of fictional characters having their residencies on Curzon Street, for example;
- Lord Henry Wotton from Oscar Wilde's The Picture of Dorian Grey.

- In one of Conan Doyle's sleuth Sherlock Holmes stories, Shoscombe Old Palace, the money lender Sam Brewer is reported as living here.
- Roald Dahl's character Henry Sugar from the Wonderful Story of Henry Sugar also lived here.
- And finally, in Agatha Christie's 'The Mystery of the Blue Train' the victim and her husband Ruth and Derek Kettering are known to have lived here, and it was down to one Hercule Poirot to solve the mystery.

Back to Real Life:

- Lady Astor reputedly lived in Curzon Street for a time, and she was the first women to sit in parliament winning her seat in the House of Commons in 1919.
- She is infamous for her verbal battles with Winston Churchill, where its alleged some of conversations went like this:
- Lady Astor said to Churchill, "If you were my husband, I'd poison your tea," to which he responded, "Madam, if you were my wife, I'd drink it."
- Another time, allegedly Lady Astor, accused Churchill of being 'disgustingly drunk' the Conservative Prime Minister responded: 'My dear, you are ugly, and what's more, you are disgustingly ugly. But tomorrow I shall be sober and you will still be disgustingly ugly

Ye Grapes

Address: 16 Shepherd Market,
Mayfair, London W1J 7QQ

Phone: 020 7493 4216

Nearest Tube: Green Park

Hours:

Sunday   12–10:30pm

Monday   11am–11pm

Tuesday   11am–11pm

Wednesday   11am–11pm

Thursday   11am–11pm

Friday   11am–11pm

Saturday   11:30am–11pm

- Ye Grapes is a grand yet small Victorian pub building set in a corner of Shepherd Market. Looking inside you will find a raft of eccentric Olde-Worlde artefacts.
- Favoured by locals for years it has in recent times gone through something of a Renaissance. It's

especially welcoming in colder times as the real fire is rather welcoming.

- This pub was established on this site in 1742 as the Market Coffee House and was renamed the Grapes in 1782. It was rebuilt in its present form in 1882.
- This is a great pub if you fancy doing the Monopoly Board Pub Crawl to end up in.

See the end of this Crawl for a Pub suggestions for a Monopoly Board Pub Crawl.

Shepherd Market:

- Developed in 1735-46 by Edward Shepherd.
- Mayfair itself is derived from the May Fair, an infamous fifteen-day gathering that took place on this site.
- James II established the fair in the 1680s, mainly for the purpose of cattle trading but soon expanded which caused some concern for Queen Anne!
- Whilst Queen Anne tried to put an end to the fair, her successor George I was more approving.
- The area then took on a more desirable entity, when 'the great and good' decided it would be a nice place to live.
- This eventually led to the fair being killed off, as more grandiose houses were erected in the 18th century.
- Since its first association with prostitutes, it appears that even today it is still so. In recent history this oldest profession was highlighted in the news when it reported that Jeffrey Archer met the prostitute Monica Coghlan here. An encounter which he tried

to cover up in a court of law, and which eventually led to his imprisonment.

- Next to Shepherd Market is Half Moon Street, where the fictional Wooster and his man servant (Valet) lived. Made famous by the novels of P.G. Wodehouse.
- Shepherd Market is a hidden respite from the storm that is London. A village within a city!

Route: Go through the Shepherd market and bear left into White Horse Street. Follow down until the junction of Piccadilly where you turn right. Stay on Piccadilly until you reach Old Park Lane on your right, turn into this and your last pub is up ahead on your right.

On your route you will enter Piccadilly, although we may have touched on some information in Crawl 4, here is a bit more!

Piccadilly

- One of the '7 noses of Soho' can be found in Piccadilly Circus.
- Just off Piccadilly, on Old Bond Street, is London's oldest chocolate shop, Charbonnel etc. Walker. However a little further down the road in Princes Arcade is another century old shop called Prestat Chocolates. One look at the window display may jog your mind about a certain film and a golden ticket. It's not such a stretch then, that if as it is claimed Roald Dahl shopped her here, maybe, just maybe, (and looking at the shop I like to think so!) some inspiration may have been gleaned from his trips here

to inspire him in his book about a young Charlie Bucket!

- Piccadilly has London's oldest bookshop; Hatchard's was established by publisher John Hatchard in 1791 at 187 Piccadilly.
- The Fortnum and Masons Clock The clock was installed on the shopfront in 1964, and contains bells cast at Whitechapel Bell Foundry. Every 15 minutes, the bells are played, and once an hour, the figures of Mr Fortnum and Mr Mason appear, and bow to each other.
- MURDER: Patricide: Millionaire business man (who owned Eastenders cash and carry in Calais was stabbed to death in a frenzied attack (2104) by his son who accused him of bullying and harassment throughout his life. And this happened in his flat just down the road in Jermyn Street. He was found with the knife still embedded in his chest!

Just across Piccadilly in Green Park next to the road in the columns which enshrine the Bomber Command Memorial.

- 55,573 young men died flying with Bomber Command during World War Two; that's more than those who serve in the entire Royal Air Force today.
- Most who flew were very young, the great majority still in their late teens. Crews came from across the globe – from the UK, Canada, Australia, New Zealand and all corners of the Commonwealth, as well as from occupied nations including Poland, France and Czechoslovakia.
- Other more specialized operations also took place. The famous 'Dam Busters' raid of May 1943 shocked the world with its audacity, as Guy Gibson's 617 Squadron launched a daring raid on the dams surrounding the Ruhr Valley.

- 1945 also saw another, lesser known mission. From 29 April to 7 May Operation Manna saw Bomber Command crews drop food supplies to the starving people of occupied Holland. Flying at 500 feet in broad daylight over hostile territory, the crews brought vital relief to the civilian population.'

  - The memorial was officially unveiled by Her Majesty the Queen on 28 June 2012.
  - Another memorial just as you go to Hyde Park Corner is the Wellington Arch. Not to be confused with Marble Arch at the other end of Park Lane.
  - This arch was first built in 1825–7, (originally another entrance to Buckingham Palace) it was moved to this position in the 1880s, and the sculpture now on top of it was only placed there in 1912.

- The subject of Adrian Jones's Quadriga (four-horse chariot), which crowns the arch, was described by Jones as 'Peace descending on the Quadriga of War'. A giant winged female figure bearing a laurel wreath descends on a great chariot, which is drawn by four rearing horses and driven by a young boy who sits on a small seat at the front of the chariot body, apparently unaware of Peace descending behind him.

Rose and Crown

Address: 2 Old Park Ln, Mayfair, London W1K 1QN

Phone: 020 7499 1980

Nearest Tube: Hyde Pk. Corner

Hours:

Sunday	12–11pm
Monday	11am–11pm
Tuesday	11am–11pm
Wednesday	11am–11pm
Thursday	11am–11pm
Friday	11am–12am
Saturday	12–11pm

- This pub has a fascinating history straddles both the Roundheads and Royalty and their times in control.

- This was once used around the time of the Civil War as accommodation for the Oliver Cromwell's bodyguards. Indeed originally called the Oliver Cromwell and stayed with that nomenclature until 1678. (You must remember that following the execution of Charles I England became a Republic for eleven years from 1649 – 1660.

- It was only after Richard Cromwell lost the confidence of Parliament in 1659 that he abdicated and Charles II returned to London and the Royal line restored. In that year it adopted its current name, and has continually provided liquid refreshment for locals since then. Indeed the Pub's sign it is the Royal Crown over the Tudor rose symbolizing the union of the houses of Lancaster and York.

The pubs location is unique as it stands very near to a famous address Number 1 London.

Number 1 London

- Apsley House at Hyde Park Corner was built in 1778 by Robert Adam for Lord Apsley, the then Lord Chancellor.

- Its location, next to the main turnpike (toll) entrance into London, gave rise to it being known as No 1 London, where central London started.

- In 1817 Apsley House was granted to the Duke of Wellington by a grateful Nation, providing him with a London residence after his victory over Napoleon at Waterloo.

- In 1819 Apsley house was redeveloped on Grand Scale, the results of which can still be seen today.

Now under the umbrella of English Heritage it is possible to visit this historical building.

Ghost Alert:

The ghost story which surrounds this property, concerns the Duke of Wellington and Oliver Cromwell (who was around nearly 200 years earlier). The tale goes that around the time of The Reform Act 1832 to which Wellesley, (Duke of Wellington) was opposed, the Duke was 'visited' by Oliver Cromwell offering his advice and guidance and warning Wellington to allow the act through Parliament. Maybe if you are lucky he may offer you some!

As this Crawl come to an end Crawl Number 6 (The Seat of Power) awaits, and the starting point is just down the road.

As an addendum to this chapter, and only due to the fact this area's anecdotes are limited, here are some items which may whet you whistle whilst you are either contemplating your journey home, or your progression onto Crawl 6. All whilst finishing off your libation!

Origins of words, phrases or sayings:

Big Wig: In the English courts of Law, both barristers and judges wear hair pieces (wigs!). The judge however wears the largest hairpiece which symbolises the most important person.

Spitting Image: In times gone by, people in the southern states of America, would when describing a boy as his 'father's son', that is he looked and acted like his dad would call him the 'spirit and image' of his father. It would appear then the term 'spitting image' is a bastardisation of 'spirit and image!'

Upper Crust: In medieval times, just like now some people struggle to make ends meet. Back then housewives would have to find ingenious ways of making the family budget stretch. One trick they used was when making a pie, they would use two types of flour, the more expensive (wheat flour) would be used on the top of the pie, and the less expensive (rye flour) would be used underneath, this then became synonymous when describing those who were well off and those who were not.

Born with a silver spoon in his/her mouth: Initially spoons were made of wood or iron, and later on from an assortment of different metals, some being precious metals. The spoon later on in its evolution, became an item which was used as a customary gift, especially for christenings, and by the child's Godparents. If the Godparents were wealthy they would present the child with a 'silver spoon', and those who were not that well-off opted for iron or wood! It can be seen how the expression developed.

Break a leg: It used to be believed, and maybe is still today that in the theatrical world malicious spirits would try and spoil someone's 'big moment', so in an effort to call a double bluff and try and outwit the evil spirits, fellow actors and well-wishers would (whilst secretly wishing for success), exclaim 'break a leg'. This then would confuse the spirit, in that, if the spirit felt success was to break a leg (as exclaimed by fellow actors), then for them to mess it up would mean them protecting the actor! Weird!

In conclusion, as mentioned earlier some of you may feel the urge to undertake a pilgrimage (that's what it would be!) and try and complete the Monopoly Board Pub Crawl. Below is a list of the places on the board and I have even searched out some of the pubs you could use. The travel could be a challenge in itself, be it bus, train, tube or taxi and is definitely not for the feint hearted.

Some or the places on the board may not have direct places within London such as Free Parking, so I have used some poetic licence in my suggestions.

Suggestions for Monopoly Board Pub Crawl (original London Board).

Whitechapel Road:	The Blind Beggar (337 Whitechapel Rd, London E1 1BU)
Old Kent Road:	The Lord Nelson (386 Old Kent Rd, London SE1 5AA)
Euston Road:	The Rocket (120 Euston Road, London NW1 2AL)
The Angel, Islington:	The Angel (3-5 Islington High St, Islington, London N1 9LQ)
Pentonville Road:	The Lexington (96-98 Pentonville Rd, London N1 9JB)
Whitehall:	The Silver Cross (33 Whitehall SW1A 2BX)
Electric Company:	Electricity Showroom (39A Hoxton Square, Shoreditch, London N1 6NN)
Northumberland Ave:	The Sherlock Holmes (10 Northumberland St, WC2N 5DB)
Pall Mall:	The Red Lion (23 Crown Passage, St James's, London SW1Y 6PP)
Bow Street:	The Marquis of Angelsea (39 Bow St, London WC2E 7AU)

Marlborough Street:	The Coach and Horses (Great Marlborough St, London W1F)
Vine Street:	The Emperor Wine Bar (35 Vine St, London EC3N 2PX)
Strand	The Coal Hole (91-92 Strand, London WC2R 0DW)
Fleet Street:	Ye Olde Cheshire Cheese (145 Fleet St, London EC4A 2BU)
Trafalgar Square:	The Admiralty (66 Trafalgar Square, St James's, London WC2N 5DS)
Leicester Square:	The Moon Under Water (28 Leicester Square, London WC2H 7LE)
Coventry Street:	The Comedy Pub (7 Oxendon St, London SW1Y 4EE)
Water Works:	The Dickins Inn (A Working Dock (water) London E1W 1UH
Piccadilly:	The Rose and Crown (2 Old Park Ln, Mayfair, London W1K 1QN)
Go to Jail:	The Rake (14 Winchester Walk, London SE1 9AG near to The Clink!)
Regent Street:	Callaghan's Irish Bar (24 Glasshouse St, Soho W1B 5)

Oxford Street:	Harry Gordons Bar (Selfridges 400 Oxford St, London W1A 1AB)
Bond Street:	The Running Horse (50 Davies St, Mayfair, London W1K 5JE)
Park Lane:	The Red Bar (Grosvenor House, 86-90 Park Ln, London W1K 7TL)
Mayfair:	Ye Grapes (16 Shepherd Market, Mayfair, London W1J 7QQ)
The 4 Stations	Pubs near the Stations
Kings Cross:	The Betjeman Arms (53 St Pancras Intl Stn, London N1C 4QL)
Fenchurch Street:	Crutched Friar (39 – 41 Crutched Friars, London EC3N 2AE)
Marylebone:	Victoria and Albert (Unit 11, Melcombe Place, London MW1 6JJ)
Liverpool Street:	Dirty Dicks (202 Bishopsgate, London EC2M 4NR) Well that concludes our Crawl around Mayfair, and it would not be right to leave without some words of wisdom!

"Here's to alcohol, the cause of, and solution to, all life's problems."

~ The Simpsons

Crawl Number 6
Westminster (The Seat of Power)

(NB: Some of these pubs are closed on Saturdays and Sundays, check before you start your crawl!)

Probably the second place on most tourists list to visit after the Tower of London, yet most tourists will probably miss the little 'snip bits' which will be laid before you on your march around the bars of Westminster and Lambeth. From Shakespeare's performances at The Palace of Whitehall to the Archbishop of Canterbury residence across the river in Lambeth, this is a crawl through the very heart of England.

From the tomb of the Unknown British Warrior in Westminster Abbey

Beneath this stone lies the body
of a British warrior
Unknown by name or rank
brought from France to lie among
the most illustrious of the land
and buried here on Armistice Day
11 Nov: 1920, in the presence of
His Majesty King George V
His Ministers of State
the Chiefs of his Forces
and a vast concourse of the nation
Thus are commemorated the many

Multitudes who during the Great
War of 1914 – 1918 gave the most that
Man can give life itself
For God
For King and country
For loved ones home and empire
For the sacred cause of justice an
The freedom of the world
They buried him among the kings because he
Had done good toward God and toward
His house

Pubs on your route:
**Bag of Nails – The Albert – The Buckingham Arms – Two
Chairman Public House – St Stephens tavern – The Fire
Station – The Horse and Stables – The Windmill Pub
(Approximately 3.2 miles)**

So Off We Go!

Bag of Nails

Address: 6 Buckingham Palace Rd, London
SW1W 0PP
Nearest Tube: Victoria
Phone: 020 7828 7003
Hours:

Wednesday	11am–11pm
Thursday	11am–11pm
Friday	11am–11pm
Saturday	11am–10:30pm
Sunday	11am–10:30pm
Monday	11am–11pm
Tuesday	11am–11pm

Conflicting reports exist about what the original pub was named or known as but we do know that it was known as, locally, 'The Devil and Bag o' Nails. It was also known as the

Bacchanals! Due to the original pub sign, which showed a satyr with cloven feet being painted black (known as the Devil by common people). The name of the tavern was only formally changed from the Devil & Bag O Nails as late as 1905.

Bacchanals:

The Bacchanalia were Roman festivals of Bacchus, the Greco-Roman god of wine, freedom, intoxication and ecstasy.

Buckingham Palace: It would be remiss not to mention the seat of her Majesty which is just behind the bag of Nails pub, whilst you may wish to visit on another day here are a few little-known facts about the palace.

- Before the Norman Conquest Edward the Confessor owned the village where the palace now stands, following that. William the Conqueror gave the site to Geoffrey de Mandeville, who in turn left it to the monks of Westminster Abbey.
- Henry VIII reclaimed it for the Crown in 1531, which brought the site of Buckingham Palace back into royal hands for the first time since William the Conqueror had given it away almost 500 years earlier.
- John Sheffield became the Duke of Buckingham in 1703, and he built Buckingham House as a place to stay during his visits to London.
- The house passed into Royal hands in 1761. It became a royal residence when King George III purchased it in 1761, for £21000 (3+ million today) as a comfortable family home for his wife, Queen Charlotte.
- It was given the ultimate makeover and transformed into a palace in 1820 by architect

John Nash – who was subsequently fired for going over his budget!

- However, Queen Victoria was the first monarch to name it as her official residence when she moved there after her coronation in 1837.
- Victoria was visited by an unusual admirer on a few occasions.
- Referred to as 'the boy Jones', teenager Edward Jones was caught in the palace three times during her reign. He was even caught red handed with her underwear stuffed into his trousers. The government eventually caught him and sent him to Brazil. He eventually escaped and returned to Blighty, but was recaptured and imprisoned on a ship for six years then sent him to Australia. Once his time was served he went on to work as a town crier before his death on Boxing Day 1893.
- Apart from the queen and her family there are 800 members of staff that live there.
- Just as an add-on, the palace contains 350 clocks and watches! They're wound up every week by two watchmen/women, who work full-time to keep them working.
- The largest palace room is over 36m long, 18m wide and 13.5m high. It's not all ballrooms and banquet halls, though: there's a whole raft of other services contained within the palace, such as a post office, police station, cinema and swimming pool, and even an onsite doctor's surgery.
- The only monarch to be born and die at Buckingham Palace was Edward VII (born 1841, died 1910).

- The Queen gave birth to Prince Charles and Prince Andrew at Buckingham Palace.
- Showing solidarity with Londoners, during World War II, King George VI and Queen Elizabeth publicly refused to leave the palace. This had a double effect, it stoked the bulldog spirit of Londoners but it also made it a high value target for the Luftwaffe.
- As a consequence, the buildings and grounds suffered multiple hits during the blitz. One such strike caused the Queen Mother to describe the bomb as causing 'a tremendous explosion' but added with a grin that 'everybody remained wonderfully calm'.
- On 8 March 1941 PC Steve Robertson, a policeman on duty at the Palace, was killed by flying debris when a bomb hit.
- The palace's 760 windows are cleaned every six weeks.
- Apparently, it is built over a range of secret tunnels.
- It is alleged that Queen Mother and King George VI loved to explore, and apparently on one such exploration they came across a young man from Newcastle who had taken to living there.
- How you can tell if the Queen is home? Well, if the Union Flag is flying she is not in, but if the Royal Standard is, she is at home.
- If see a Royal Standard flying from Victoria Tower at the Palace of Westminster, this means the Queen is in Parliament.

Fire

- On June 2nd 2002, there was a fire at Buckingham Palace which was the eve of the Queen's Golden Jubilee weekend celebrations.
- It was caused by an electric heater brought in to tackle dry rot.
- The fire started broke out above the East Gallery in the west wing of the Palace as performers rehearsed for the Party at the Palace pop concert.
- It was found to be accidental and in a joint statement the Fire brigade and police said "The cause of the fire was found to be the ignition of rot mould which caught fire in the drying out process during dry rot treatment."
- Eric Clapton, Phil Collins and Brian May had to be evacuated from the Palace with Royal staff and concert organisers.
- More than 100 firefighters eventually brought the flames under control after about 75 minutes.
- Damage was limited by the actions of the Fire Service and the fire compartmentation.

Ghost alert:
The Chained Monk – Buckingham Palace

- Long before Buckingham Palace, the Monks of Westminster Abbey had a priory which stood on the site and was then surrounded by marshland.
- So it is asserted that the Chained Monk which visits on Christmas Day it is the ghost of a monk who died in the monastery's cells (no one is sure what he had done to warrant the chains etc.).
- He appears on the terrace over the gardens to the rear of the building.

Loves Labour Lost

- Another ghost which frequents the Palace is that of Major John Gwynne (Born 9 November 1841 – Died 6 May 1910). He was King Edward VII's private secretary and became divorced from his wife whilst still in service.
- At the time this was a considered to be a scandal, no record can be found as to why he was divorced, but he became disavowed from the higher echelons of society.
- Fearing no way back, he went to bed one night with his hand gun and killed himself. The gun shot has since been heard on many occasions by people in the area where he killed himself.

Route: Come out of the pub and crossover the main road and go down Bressenden Place. At the junction with Victoria Street turn left and head down this street past all the glass high rise buildings until you come across your next watering hole on your left, The Albert.

On your route: as you pass down Victoria Street look on your right and you will see Westminster Cathedral.

- The Cathedral site was originally known as Bulinga Fen and formed part of the marsh around Westminster.
- It was reclaimed by the Benedictine monks who were the builders and owners of Westminster Abbey.
- After the reformation the land was used in turn as a maze, a pleasure garden and as a ring for bull-baiting but it remained largely waste ground.

- In the 17th century a part of the land was sold by the Abbey for the construction of a prison which was demolished and replaced by an enlarged prison complex in 1834.
- The site was acquired by the Catholic Church in 1884.
- The Cathedral Church of Westminster, which is dedicated to the Most Precious Blood of Our Lord Jesus Christ, was designed in the Early Christian Byzantine style by the Victorian architect John Francis Bentley.
- The foundation stone was laid in 1895 and the fabric of the building was completed eight years later.

Before the Cathedral

- Prior to the Cathedral a prison stood on this site.
- Tothill Fields Bridewell prison was located in this area between 1618 and 1884. Tothill Fields later became the Westminster House of Correction.
- It was knocked down in 1836, two years after the new prison opened,
- The Tothill Fields Prison of 1834 was built in the form of a shamrock; each part forming a separate prison.
- Each of the three prison parts contained about 300 prisoners, one for the boys and the other two for women.
- Although it was set up to take people who had less harsh sentences, after 1850 it was decided it would only be for kids below 17 years old, effectively becoming a Children's prison.

- The oldest boy in 1861 was eighteen, having lied about his age to get in.
- Woken by the sound of a gun, the boys then followed a strict regime, a brisk cold wash to start followed by Chapel and breakfast. Gruel seemed to be the meal of choice at that time.
- Some kids were imprisoned for the heinous crimes of playing 'knock down ginger' and spinning a top in public!
- The girl's prison has less information readily available but we do know they were committed for crimes such as non-payment of fines and one girl for stealing boots! See photo under Westminster Abbey.** With acknowledgments to Henry Mayhew's "Criminal Prisons of London".

Ghost Alert

- The Cathedral is apparently haunted by a ghostly Cleric, dressed in black robes and is seen 'hanging' about at the High Altar.
- The last documented sighting was back in 1966, when a parish worker, working late into the night saw the 'black robed priest' appear right in front of him, as he continued to stare in disbelief the ghostly image faded away.

The Albert

Address: 52 Victoria St, London SW1H 0NP
Nearest Tube: St James Park
Phone: 020 7222 5577
Hours:

Wednesday	11am–11pm
Thursday	11am–12am
Friday	11am–12am
Saturday	10am–11pm
Sunday	11am–10:30pm
Monday	11am–11pm
Tuesday	11am–11pm

- A true survivor from the Victorian Era, originally known as The Blue Coat Boy, and was built between 1845 -1852. The name change came about in honour of Queen Victoria's husband, The Prince Consort.
- In 1862 it was bought for just £978!
- It's worth a visit to look at the collectable curios, which include Queen Victoria's napkin, the

Prime Minsters' Gallery and an original Parliamentary Division Bell, once rang to notify government ministers to rush to vote.

Route: Come out of the pub and turn left into Buckingham Gate. Continue along here until you reach Petty France on your right. Turn down here and proceed down Petty France until you see our next pub, The Buckingham Arms on your right.

Not much of note between the next two pubs apart from Wellington Barracks, but as there is a lot to do coming up after this interlude, enjoy the walk. Rather than make you walk all the way without a stop before we hit the mother lode, I have found a couple of pubs to stop off at to break up the walk.

Buckingham Arms

Address: 62 Petty France, SW1H 9EU
Nearest Tube: St James Park
Phone: 020 7222 3386
Hours:

Wednesday	11am–11pm
Thursday	11am–11pm
Friday	11am–11pm
Saturday	11am–6pm
Sunday	11am–6pm
Monday	11am–11pm
Tuesday	11am–11pm

Yet another an example of a traditional Victorian pub built in the early 1800s. Like some other pubs in this crawl this is not in a very tourist area, but is only a stone's throw from the Palace.

Historically the pub was named after the well-loved George Villiers (especially by King James 1st ...allegedly), and it was he who had the title 1st Duke of Buckingham. One of the richest men in England, was also well known for his arrogance, and the comment made by me earlier, about him being 'well-loved' may have been true about the affection shown him by King James I, but out in the real world this did not hold him in a great favour with the public, In fact, the Duke was stabbed to death, on 23 August 1628, at the Greyhound Pub in Portsmouth. Aged just 36!

Route: Turn Right out of the pub and continue along Petty France and carry straight on into Broadway and Tothill Street, then take the left turn into Dartmouth Street and our nest stop The Two chairman is down there on your right.

Two Chairman Public House

Address: 39 Dartmouth St, SW1H 9BP
Nearest Tube: St James Park
Phone: 020 7222 8694
Hours:

Wednesday	12–11pm
Thursday	12–11pm
Friday	12–11pm
Saturday	Open 24 hours
Sunday	Open 24 hours
Monday	12–11pm
Tuesday	12–11pm

- Traced back to 1729 and located just opposite the infamous early theatre The Royal Cockpit, which was built on a site originally acquired by Henry VIII, and was known for its cockfighting arena.
- Reputedly called the Two Chairmen after two sedan carrying men who would wait in the pub for their wealthy patrons who were at the cockfighting! Much like a modern day Taxi or Uber ☺.

- One popular belief is that when wanting to 'hail' a sedan chair, the prospective fare would shout "Chair Ho" and that this is the evolution of the word "cheerio!"
- The sedan chair was originally brought to England in the 17th Century and was popular with wealthy people who did not want to walk through the dirty, smelly, muddy streets of London at that time.
- Originating from a town of the same name in France 'Sedan'. First introduced, albeit for a short period by the Duke of Buckingham in the early 1600s (see Buckingham Arms above).
- This did not help his public persona, as they felt he was using men to animals work! They were brought back in 1634 by Sir Saunders Duncombe, who attained a license to provide sedan for the public.
- They quickly became popular, as they were cheaper and provided head space and cover for the extravagant wigs of the time.
- This is also supposed to be the oldest pub in Westminster.

Route:

Come out of pub and turn right which follows around into Old Queen Street at the end of the street, turn left into Storey's Gate, then right into Great George Street which leads you past Parliament Square. Carry on straight forward and you will see St Stephens Tavern on your left

Right here we go again! Be prepared for lots of info coming up!

As you pass Parliament Square some brief points about the Houses of Parliament (Palace of Westminster), and Westminster Abbey which will be on your right.

Houses of Parliament (Palace Of Westminster)

- Parliament is divided into two chambers. The House of Commons and the House of Lords.
- In the House of Lords, red is the primary colour employed in upholstery, notepaper; etc. The choice of colour is relatively easy to explain as it probably stems from the use by kings of red as a royal colour and its consequent employment in the room where the King met his court and nobles.
- In the House of Commons the choice of green as its primary colour is a bit more circumspect.
- One theory is that as the theatres in London began to adopt the use of green in the late 1600s for items such as seats curtains etc. (Indeed, the term Green room is still used today as a place where actors etc. took respite before, and after shows.) As Parliament was seen as theatre in which debates took place, and theatres were entertainment for 'common people' as well as the well off, it's easy to see why green was adopted for the commons!
- The first authoritative mention of the use of green in the Chamber in the House of Commons was in 1663.
- Some strange customs and traditions still are practiced today, such as when a new 'speaker of

the House' is elected they have to be physically dragged to their seat.

- This may be down to the fact that in the early days of Parliament their role was to communicate information from the commons to the King/Queen, and guess what happened if they did not like to information! So it may been seen to be a bit of a poisoned chalice, and therefore needed some 'support' to take the job.

- Seven Speakers between 1394 and 1535 were executed, killed in battle, or murdered.

- The only speaker who became a Saint and Martyr was Sir Thomas More, Speaker in 1523, and executed in 1535 for refusing to swear the oath declaring Henry VIII to be the head of the church.

- You may have heard about a woolsack in the House of Lords, well this is used by the Lord Speaker, and is in effect a red cushion originally stuffed with English Wool.

- It was introduced by King Edward III (1327-77) as a reminder that the wool trade was one of England's main source of wealth.

- The use of the gold mace is to open parliament. It is not to be touched except by the bearer.

- In recent years this rule has been abused, once by Michael Heseltine who picked it up and waved it threateningly at the Labour opposition (1976).

- In 1987 Ron Brown (Labour MP) through it in the floor in a fit of rage, and had to pay £1500 for its repair.

- If you watch on TV, there are two lines separating the parties across the house. Supposedly they are set two sword lengths apart so you cannot reach the other side with a single lunge.

- MPs are also forbid to cross those lines which prevent physical violence! Maybe some other parliaments around the world should adopt this!
- It is alleged as well that there are secret tunnels under Parliament, one is which is believed to be true is one which links Parliament with Downing Street.
- Also there is a rifle range somewhere in the basement.
- Other oddities include; a snuffbox by the front door of the Commons. It's been there for centuries and it's always full of snuff.
- Black Rod (a Lords Chamber Officer) is sent from the Lords Chamber to the Commons Chamber to summon MPs to hear the Queen's Speech. Traditionally the door of the Commons is slammed in Black Rod's face to symbolise the Commons independence.
- He then bangs three times on the door with the rod. The door to the Commons Chamber is then opened and all MPs – talking loudly – follow Black Rod back to the Lords to hear the Queen's Speech.
- This knocking has gone on since the last monarch to enter the House of Commons was King Charles I, in 1642. Charles flounced in with his curly locks in the air and his rather nice moustache twitching in a petulant rage when he was seeking to arrest five Members of Parliament on charges of high treason.

- There is a toilet behind an old oak panel in the commons where MPs apparently, who were too scared of the whips and didn't want to vote, hid.
- One of the copies of the Magna Carta is hanging framed on the wall; it's the closest we get to a constitution in the UK. I've seen one of the other copies in Salisbury cathedral.

Fire:

- On 16 October 1834 at about 6.30 pm, a fire broke out in the Palace after an overheated stove used to destroy the Exchequer's stockpile of tally sticks, led to a huge fireball and set fire to the House of Lords Chamber. The conflagration that followed destroyed both Houses of Parliament, and the surrounding buildings.
- Westminster Hall was only saved due to the local fire-fighting efforts, which were aided, at just the right time, by a change in wind direction.
- It should be noted that The London Fire Brigade did not exist back in 1834.
- Before the London Fire Brigade, which formed in London had, ten independent fire insurance companies united in 1833 to form the London Fire Engine Establishment (LFEE) to provide the public with a more resourceful and effective fire service.
- James Braidwood, an experienced firefighter from Edinburgh, held the role of Superintendent and it was he who was in charge that fateful night.
- Thousands gathered to watch the spectacle, and volunteers manned the pumps all night But their

efforts were failing, and firefighters soon realised they had to prioritise their efforts.

- It is said that Viscount Althorp, then chancellor of the Exchequer said "Damn the House of Commons... but save, o save [Westminster] Hall."
- Guess what? The hall indeed survived, but most of rest of the complex lay in ruins the next morning.

Westminster Abbey

- Westminster Abbey is built close to where a vision of St Peter is said to have been seen on the Thames by a salmon fisherman named Edric.
- The Fishermen's Company offers a salmon to Westminster Abbey each year in memory of this. (See below about liveries).
- The abbey was originally titled the Collegiate Church of St Peter at Westminster.
- It is not an abbey. Officially it is a Royal Peculiar, a church responsible directly to the sovereign.
- Edward the Confessor rebuilt it starting around 1042 as a burial place for English kings (17 Monarchs have been buried here).
- All coronations have been held at the abbey since those of Harold Godwinson in January 1066 and William the Conqueror in December 1066.
- There has also been 16 royal weddings have been held here, although only two were reigning Kings at the time of their nuptials (Henry I and Richard II).
- Although Oliver Cromwell was granted a funeral here in 1658, Charles II on his return to the

demanded that Cromwell be punished for his crimes of high treason and regicide. And so Cromwell's body was exhumed, along with John Bradshaw, President of the High Court of Justice for the trial of King Charles I to be posthumously killed. The date of the execution was chosen as it was the anniversary of King Charles I own death, 12 years earlier.

- The bodies were hung and then beheaded at sunset and thrown into an unmarked pit.

- The heads were put on a spike at Westminster Hall, where they stayed on display for more than 20 years. (I think the King had a grudge, but I could be wrong!)

- The heads only came down because a storm broke the spike and sent the heads tumbling down.

- Only one person is buried in the standing position and that is the poet Ben Johnson, reputedly, he told the Dean of the Abbey: "six feet long by two feet wide is too much for me. Two feet by two is all I want".

- Another 'special' tomb is that of the Unknown Warrior (from WWI), what makes it extra special is that it's the only tomb that CANNOT be walked on.

- On the 11 November 1920 the complete but unidentified remains of a World War I soldier was given a Royal Funeral and buried in soil especially bought from the battlefields of France, and now lies under a marble stone quarried from Belgium in the Abbey.

- A usual statue is that of Saint Wilgefortis, why unusual? This is the only statue of a women with a beard in the abbey!
- Her story: Recalling the legend, the father of a young noblewoman named Wilgefortis had been promised in marriage to a pagan king. Not wanting to wed this man, and that she had taken a vow of virginity, she prayed to be made repulsive. Her prayers were answered, and she grew a lovely beard! Result, the pagan king would not want her now, however her father was so enraged he had her crucified.
- The Abbey has a ring of ten bells which was dedicated in 1971.
- The tenor bell has a diameter of 4 feet 6 inches (137 cm), weighing 1,530 kg, and is tuned to the note of D.
- The tenor bell has a special function as it is tolled following the announcement of the death of Royal family member and on the death of the Dean of Westminster.
- The College garden is one of the oldest gardens in England, and was used by the Benedictine Monks to grow herbs and food which was considered to combat ailments.

Sited in Little George Street (near the Abbey) stands the only original piece of Tothill Fields prison still in existence.

Fire

- The Abbey did not escape the Blitz, on the night of 10/11 May 1941 clusters of incendiaries (fire bombs rather than high explosives) fell on the roof and nearby.
- Due to an organised team of fire watchers and volunteers a lot them were dealt with efficiently.
- One however landed on the lantern roof, at the centre of the Abbey, due to its position it was hard to reach and eventually burned through the lead and took hold on a beam.
- As London was under siege, water supplies were very low across the capital and as a consequence the fire took hold, sending flames 40 feet into the air.
- It was however quite lucky that it did burn where it did, because the timbers and beams when they failed, fell into the open space below and the fires were easily dealt with.
- Some surrounding buildings were also affected.

Ghost Alert

- Stabbed to death during a robbery, this tall, thin monk has been known to make an appearance in full view of the public. Affectionately known as Father Benedictus, he has been seen to hover just above the floor and has even talked with the Abbey's visitors. Reports from the early 1900s suggest he has conversed with groups of people on numerous occasions.

- The second spectre to reside in the Abbey is an unknown soldier. He stands by the tomb of the Unknown Warrior; his mouth moves as if he is trying to talk, but no sound emerges.

Just before you reach the next pub on your left is Whitehall, and here are a couple of factoids for you.

- Just down Whitehall on the right is the place where The Palace of Whitehall (or Palace of White Hall) stood, and this was the main residence of the English monarchs in London from 1530 until 1698.
- The name Whitehall or White Hall was first recorded in 1532; it had its origins in the white stone used for the buildings.
- Henry VIII married two of his wives at the palace—Anne Boleyn in 1533 and Jane Seymour in 1536. Henry died at the palace in January 1547. In 1611 the palace hosted the first known performance of William Shakespeare's play *The Tempest.*
- The English Civil War (1642-1651) went back and forth until the defeat at the Battle of Preston of Charles 1st's army in August 1648.
- Oliver Cromwell had the King charged with high treason against the realm of England. During the trial, Charles refused to accept the authority of the court and did not enter a plea. Nevertheless, the court found him guilty and he was sentenced to death.
- Three days later, the king was led to the scaffold erected at Whitehall, London.
- There is a memorial plaque/bust on a building in Whitehall which shows the place he was executed.

- A major fire on the 4th January 1698 brought to an end the days of the palace except for the Banqueting House which was saved.

- New regulations had been implemented in 1662 in an effort to reduce the risk of fire (this stipulated that there should be one leather bucket filled with water for each chimney).

- However, the Palace had a precursor to the later fire. In 1691, a similar fire started in the Duchess of Portsmouth's lodgings almost destroying the palace, but through the actions of the staff the fire was contained.

- But seven years later, some linen left to dry by a charcoal fire caught light and within five hours almost the whole palace was destroyed.

- In trying to save the palace, Servants, Courtiers and workmen all got in the way of one another, (one group trying to salvage the art, one group locking doors to prevent looting, and finally the workman trying to create a fire break by destroying some parts of the building) and in their confusion contributed to the destruction of the Palace.

- Over the next twenty-years various monarch tried to resurrect the Palace, but the treasury was low on funds and so it never got past the wishing stage.

Just down the road now to our next watering hole!

St Stephens Tavern

Address: 10 Bridge St, London SW1A
2JR
Nearest tube: Westminster
Phone: 020 7925 2286
Hours:

Wednesday	10am–11:30pm
Thursday	10am–11:30pm
Friday	10am–11:30pm
Saturday	10am–11:30pm
Sunday	10:30am–10:30pm
Monday	10am–11:30pm
Tuesday	10am–11:30pm

A Grade II listed pub which had been closed for nearly 15 years before reopening in 2003. This 125-year-old pub is believed to have been frequented by many 'A lister's' of the time including prime ministers such as Baldwin, Churchill and Macmillan, who it is said used to pop in now and again for a 'lemonade'!

The obvious location next to Parliament meant that the clientele may have come out of work (Parliament) for a quick libation, and so not to miss out on any vote a Division Bell was mounted on the wall above the bar. This device, has been in use for over 150 years, and used to summon Members of Parliament back to the House of Commons for a vote, or 'division'. When the bell sounds the MPs have just eight minutes to dash back to the House of Commons, or risk the wrath of their Party leaders. Some other local establishments have a division bell as well, but the time scale for return may have been a bit harder to achieve. It may still be in use today, so if you hear what appears to be an alarm, whilst you are in there, have a look to see if anyone runs out the door.

NOTE: Make sure it's not the FIRE ALARM!

Route:

Turn left out of the pub and cross over Westminster Bridge, before the roundabout turn left down York Road, continue on this road until you reach the IMAX roundabout. Here you are going to turn right and walk down Waterloo Road, The Fire Station pub is down here under the Railway Bridge on your right.

On your route:

As you leave the pub look to your right and you will see St Stephens Tower which was erected during the mid-1800s, mistakenly people believe it is called Big Ben, when it is only the bell (13 tons) that is called Big Ben, and this was named after the Commissioner of works, Sir Benjamin Hall, who was by all accounts a very large man.

3 special anniversaries for Big Ben

- Big Ben was cast on 10th April 1858.
- The clock is called The Great Westminster Clock and started working on 31st May 1859.

- Big Ben first chimed the hour on 11th July 1859.
- Big Ben of today was not the first Big Ben!
- The original bell was cast on 6 August 1856 in Stockton-on-Tees.
- Since St Stephens Tower was not yet finished, the bell was mounted in New Palace Yard.
- The first bell was transported to the tower on a trolley drawn by sixteen horses, with crowds cheering its progress.
- During the bell's testing, it cracked beyond repair and a replacement had to be made.
- The new Big Ben was recast on 10 April 1858 at the Whitechapel Bell Foundry.

You may have heard also that a few years back in 1605 some people tried to blow up the House of Parliament!

This event became affectionately known as the Gun Powder Plot.

13 people were at the heart of this conspiracy, which came about because of the persecution of Catholics in Protestant England which was being ruled by King James I at the time.

Remember, remember the fifth of November, Gunpowder treason and plot. We see no reason why gunpowder treason should ever be forgot! Guy Fawkes, guy, t'was his intent. To blow up king and parliament. Three score barrels were laid below. To prove old England's overthrow. By god's mercy he was catch'd. With a darkened lantern and burning match. So, holler boys, holler boys, Let the bells ring. Holler boys, holler boys, God save the king. And what shall we do with him? Burn Him!

- Ironically Guido Fawkes was not the ring leader, yet it is he we all remember for this attempt to blow up the House of Lords at the State Opening of

Parliament on 5 November 1605, while the king and many other important members of the aristocracy and nobility were inside.

- Henry VIII is mainly responsible for changing England from a Catholic country to a Protestant one, when he declared himself head of the Church in England in 1834, after he was excommunicated in 1833 by Pope Paul III.
- When his daughter Elizabeth I became Monarch, she continued to promote the Protestant agenda so much so that by her death in 1603, Catholics were forced to celebrate Mass in secret in private houses (this led to the tradition of why candles are in the windows at Christmas, as they were used as a sign to show a mass was being celebrated within.)
- Catholics were also forced to attend Protestant Services to try and convert them.
- Despite being married to Catholic James I, continued with the persecution of Catholics and his increased penalties on those who openly declared or celebrated Catholicism led to the plot being hatched.
- Led by Robert Catesby the plot was discussed initially on the 20th May 1604 in a London inn. Eventually the group expanded to 13 people.
- Lord Monteagle (House of Lords) received an anonymous letter on the 26th October 1605, in which it advised him that it may be better for him to be absent from the opening of Parliament, feeling this was important and passed the information to King James I, this then led the King to come to the conclusion it was a plan to blow up the Houses of Parliament.

- So additional secret measures were taken, and low and behold on the 5th, poor old Guy Fawkes was caught red handed!
- After the King gave permission to use torture, Guy Fawkes gave up his fellow conspirators and admitted their part in it.
- The remaining plotters were held up in *Staffordshire*, where several, including Catesby, died in a shoot-out with the king's men.
- Those that survived and Guy Fawkes were finally hung, drawn and quartered in January 1606.

On your route over Westminster Bridge (note that it is painted green like the House of Commons).

Whilst crossing the River Thames pause for thought! It may look nice today with the boats moving back and forth, but this was not always the case!

The Great Stench (1858)

- The summer of 1858 was excessively and with that came a smell which nigh on brought London to its knees.
- People were even reluctant to leave their homes.

- For years the river was a dumping ground for waste of all types and whilst it could cope when it was a small city in Roman times, but as the population and industry expanded it became over polluted.
- So by the mid-1800s it was just a mass of who knows what!
- Well in 1858 with the heat, the sewage began to ferment so the smell became unbearable, so much so people living or working near the river suffered dramatically.
- Parliament in an effort to 'lead by example' decided to mask the stench by coating the curtains in a mixture of Chorine and Lime, but this was of no avail, and they could not move offices as that would not have looked good to those who did not have this option.
- Forced to act, they passed a bill into law within 18 days.
- This new law not only required a complete overhaul of the river, by the installation of embankments but also called a new sewage system—to be designed by the English civil engineer Sir Joseph Bazalgette.

Ghost Alert:
Westminster Bridge – The Ghost Boat & Jack the Ripper

- Stand on Westminster Bridge on a spooky night, and you may catch a glimpse of the famous ghost boat – a small vessel with three people on its deck, which has been seen passing under the bridge before disappearing.
- Some people swear that on New Year's Eve, the figure of Jack the Ripper can also be seen leaping off the bridge into the waters below.
- If you are not overly concerned about 'ringing in the New Year' by embracing someone as Big Ben herald's the New Year, then stand on Westminster Bridge, and look eastward.
- If you look carefully you may see the spectre of Jack the Ripper leaping off the edge of the bridge, re-enacting the legend that in 1888, he indeed committed suicide from this spot.
- His life of crime has been punished, in that he is forever in torment and condemned to relive his suicide every year as the bells chime midnight!

There are lots of sights as you make your way along the road but I will move directly on to the next pub, as I feel you may be a bit light-headed as you have had quite a bit of…information so far. So for now just enjoy the walk past the London Eye, Festival Hall etc.

The Fire Station

Address: 150 Waterloo Rd, SE1 8SB
Nearest Tube: Waterloo
Phone: 020 3727 5938
Hours:

Wednesday	7am–11pm
Thursday	7am–12am
Friday	7am–12am
Saturday	9am–12am
Sunday	9am–10:30pm
Monday	7am–11pm
Tuesday	7am–11pm

Previously an Operational Fire station, but nowadays a Public House.

- There were two Waterloo Rd fire stations. The old LFEE station closed in 1872, then reopened in 1876. Replaced by a new building on an adjacent site in 1910.

- 150 Waterloo Road was built in 1910 as Waterloo Road Fire Station for the London County Council.
- Closed 1937 when the HQ at Lambeth opened. Reopened during WW2 as a sub-station. Closed 1945.
- By 1986 its original use had ceased, and the building had become the headquarters of the London Ambulance Service.
- The latter subsequently transferred its headquarters to a new building further down Waterloo Road; no. 150 is now a restaurant and bar, known as The Fire Station, with offices on the upper floors.

Route: turn right out of the pub then take the first right, bear right at the fork to stay on Bayliss Road, and continue until the junction with Westminster Bridge Road. Turn left and your next drink is awaiting you.

On your route now you can relax a bit, and give your brain a rest ready for the next onslaught following your liquid refreshment.

The Horse and Stables

Address: 124 Westminster Br. Rd, SE1 7RW
Nearest Tube: Lambeth North
Phone: 020 7928 6277
Hours:

Wednesday	12–11pm
Thursday	12–11pm
Friday	12pm–1am
Saturday	12pm–2am
Sunday	Closed
Monday	12–11pm
Tuesday	12–11pm

They are proud to say, "First and Foremost we are an English Pub".

An eccentric looking pub with an interesting inside configuration, private booths and quirky nooks, alongside comfortable furnishings all lead to a traditional English pub atmosphere.

Starting life as a pub in the late 1800s, it has been rebuilt and refurbished a few times, but although history may not be its strong selling point, it's quintessentially English in its outlook. It is also a dog friendly pub, which is quite rare in the city. Check out the function room upstairs. Never has the saying 'never judge a book by its cover' been so relevant.

On your route you will pass The Imperial War Museum and Lambeth Palace.

Imperial War museum

- What used to be the Bethlem Hospital is now the Imperial War Museum.
- The original building was the successor of the medieval hospital in the priory of St Mary of Bethlehem in Bishopsgate Without (now Liverpool Street Station).
- In 1247 the Priory of St Mary of Bethlehem was founded, devoted to healing sick paupers. The small establishment became known as Bethlehem Hospital. Londoners later abbreviated this to 'Bethlem' and often pronounced it 'Bedlam'.
- This is where the term "bedlam" has its origins, originally meaning noise and confusion; the association was made by locals who would regularly hear screaming, crying, and chains rattling etc. And the name stuck.
- The first reference to this hospital is recorded in 1329, but there is no mention of the ailments the patients suffered from.
- But in 1403 reference is made that they were suffering from mental health problems.

- This was used as a 'human zoo' and the well to do and general public would pay to visit the asylum to gawk and applaud at the patients' misfortune, much like BIG Brother on TV today ☺
- This practise of parading patients as a form of entertainment was stopped in 1770.
- The bad press which now stained the hospital forced a further move to the site in South London in 1815.
- It continued as a hospital/asylum until its conversion to the imperial War museum in 1936.

Fire:

- On 13 October 1968, the Museum was attacked by an arsonist, Timothy John Daly, (an anti-Vietnam war protester) who claimed he was acting in protest against the exhibition of militarism to children.
- It was thought the attack may have been a precursor to the London Demonstration set for October 27 1968.
- He caused damage valued at approximately £200,000, destroying the dome and the loss of irreplaceable books and documents.
- All volumes of The Illustrated London News since 1854 were also destroyed.
- On his conviction in 1969 he was sentenced to four years in prison.
- Over 100 firemen eventually brought it under control.

Doing the Lambeth Walk:

Anytime you're Lambeth way,
Any evening, any day,
You'll find us all doin' the Lambeth walk.
Every little Lambeth gal,
With her little Lambeth pal,
You'll find 'em all doin' the Lambeth walk.
Everything's free and easy,
Do as you darn well pleasey,
Why don't you make your way there,
Go there, stay there.
Once you get down Lambeth way,
Every evening, every day,
You'll find yourself doin' the Lambeth walk.

- **"The Lambeth Walk"** is actually a song from a musical (Me and My Girl).
- The song takes its name from a local street Lambeth Walk. This thoroughfare once had a thriving street market and epitomised working class culture in Lambeth.
- People not only from all over the local area but from around the world came to shop here.
- Cockneys, Rhyming Slang and Pie & Mash were introduced to the world from here, through the medium of stage and screen.
- Lambeth in the 19th century was a hub of industry, Vauxhall built their first car in Vauxhall!), with that industry came the workers, and so the population grew and grew.
- As the more and more people moved into the area, (sometimes families had 15 children all

living in 2 or 3 rooms), overcrowding led to disease spreading rapidly.

Lambeth Palace

- This Palace is the official home of the Archbishop of Canterbury, the leader of the Church of England. The line of Archbishops of Canterbury goes back more than 1,400 years.
- The oldest part of Lambeth Palace dates from the 13th century, and over the centuries the building has been added to and altered. Much of the palace's Gothic look was added in the 19th century.
- Archbishop Parker (6 August 1504 – 17 May 1575) is the only person to be buried in the Palace.
- Morton's Tower, is the main entrance to the palace (just off Lambeth Palace Road).
- "The Lambeth Dole", a daily offering of bread, broth and money was first instigated by Archbishop Winchelsea in the thirteenth century. This ritual of charitable giving was offered from Morton's Tower until 1842.

- Archbishop Laud brought a tortoise to Lambeth in 1633 as a pet. He was given this as a gift from his college at Oxford University. As they tend to do, tortoises have a long life span and ultimately outlived the Archbishop by over 100 years.
- Tragically it was killed at the age of 120, when in 1753 it was dug up out of hibernation by a Palace worker and died of frost exposure.
- The Great Hall currently houses the majority of Lambeth Palace Library, an extremely important ecclesiastical collection, second only to the Vatican. The Palace also houses a rare book conservation studio and further storage space for their 250,000 book collection.
- The palace did not escape the wrath of the Luftwaffe, and during the Blitz of the WWII it was hit with a bomb, and the scorch marks can still be seen in the chapel.

- Next door if St Mary's church, dating from the mid-1800s. I mention this as there is a significant grave there, that of Admiral William Bligh, of Mutiny on the Bounty fame.

Fire:

- 5th Dec 1897; Fire started in vestry room in Cranmer's Tower, and it attributed to one of the old beams in the chimney igniting.
- Staff and residents acted promptly and a messenger was sent to Waterloo Road Fire Station (see the Fire Station pub above).
- Superintendent G Pettit arrived on the 'steamer' and immediately set his crews to work, after an hour the fire was subdued.

Lambeth Bridge:

Did you know that Lambeth Bridge is painted Red to be in harmony with the seat colour of the House of Lords? (Green for Westminster.)

Ghost Alert

Lambeth Palace is said to be haunted by the ghost of Queen Anne Boleyn wailing and pleading for her life.

- Although history shows her trial was held in the Tower of London, and she was transported there from Greenwich Palace on 2nd May 1536, the Lambeth Palace Screaming/Crying ghost is said to be Anne Boleyn.
- However, this legend may have stemmed from the Court Hearing, concerned with the dissolution of her marriage to Henry VIII.
- This was held at Lambeth Palace by Thomas Cranmer, and in Anne's absence, as she was locked up in the tower of London.
- She was notified of the outcome that night at cell in The Tower. So maybe the crying is not just for her life but for her marriage!
- Another ghostly legend is that a local tomb states that if you dance around it twelve times as Big Ben strikes midnight then a ghost will appear; may be worth searching out! Not sure if the Archbishop of Canterbury would want you in the gardens at midnight, but if you ask nicely.

The Windmill Pub

Address: 44 Lambeth High St, SE1 7JS **Nearest Tube**: Lambeth North
Phone: 020 7820 1802
Hours:

Wednesday	12–11pm
Thursday	12–11pm
Friday	12–11pm
Saturday	Closed
Sunday	Closed
Monday	12–11pm
Tuesday	12–11pm

- This is a pub you would only have stumbled upon, if you were venturing off the beaten track.
- As with a lot of London there are plenty of hidden gems, and one of the nice things to do is just wander, and see what you discover.
- You would think that with a street name like Lambeth High Street this would be a main

thoroughfare, yet as you go along it you will see otherwise.

- This is yes another pub with character and a plethora of '*objets curieux*', it even has some fire brigade equipment on site (probably as a homage to the fire station next door).
- This site has been occupied by an inn since 1454, and the first licence was issued to John Calcot.
- The previous name was 'The Chequers'. The Windmill has been here since circa 1821, and was rebuilt around 1880.

The fire station next door was built in 1936 by the London County Council. Nowadays the headquarters have moved to Union Street (near Waterloo), but the Fire station and River station remain.

Fire:

30 January 1918

A dark day in the London Fire Brigades history. Although technically WWI was still ongoing (28 Jul 1914 – 11 Nov 1918), this fire was considered to be the greatest single loss London Firefighters in 'peacetime London.

Place: Three Storey Pepper Mills, Albert Embankment.

Date: Wednesday 30th January 1918

Time: 03:44 (sunrise was due at 07:43)

Cause: Unknown but presumed to be rats gnawing through electrical cables.

- The brigade attendance over the next two hours consisted of three fire engines and an escape ladder. With some 25 firefighters and officers attending the scene.
- Weather conditions were poor, dense fog, coupled with the smoke contributed to the

visibility being very poor and did not help efforts the to deal with the fire.

- It was around 0545 when Brigade Superintendent Barrow heard the building crack and shouted to everyone "drop everything and run" as the building started to collapse.(see prose below).
- I do not normally mention people by name but feel these unsung heroes deserve a mention as on that fateful day they all lost their lives.
- Sub-officer William E. Cornford (Clapham), Fireman Edmund J. Fairbrother (Kennington), Fireman William E. Nash (Kennington), Fireman John .W.C. Johnson (Vauxhall), Fireman Aurther A. Page (Vauxhall) and Temp. Fireman James E. Fay (Kennington) were all killed by falling debris when the front of the building collapsed.
- Sub-Officer Walter W. Hall (Vauxhall) was severely injured and later died in St Thomas's Hospital.

Below is an extract which makes chilling reading from the Brigades official record

From – Superintendent the Divisional Officer, "E" District Southern Division. 30th January 1918.

Loss of Life at a Fire – Collapse of Building

I submit that at 3-44 a.m. of this date a call was received by stranger to a private house alight at Albert Embankment, S.E., to which Motor Escape, Motor Pump and ten men from No.94. Station Vauxhall and Motor Pump and six men from No.87. Station Kennington responded.

At 3-55 a.m., a "home call" message was received, viz:- It is a building of three floors about 40 x 40 ft. used as Pepper Mills alight, one hydrant in use. No.3. Westminster Motor

Pump and six men were ordered and I attended with No.80. Motor Car and two men.

On my arrival I found the upper floors of a building of three floors about 45 x 30 ft. (used as cattle food manufacturers) well alight, and part of roof and upper floor had fallen in.

The fire was practically extinguished by the use of two hydrants and one Motor Pump and the stop sent back accordingly.

At 5-34 a.m., owing to a considerable amount of turning over to be done, a message was dispatched to the effect that appliances would be detained for a time and a few minutes later another message asking or a Sub-officer and four men to be sent on with a view to the appliances and myself returning home.

At about 5-45 a.m. I was on the ground floor and in consequence of hearing a cracking noise, cleared everyone out of the building.

Owing to the ground mist and smoke, the front of the building was hardly discernible, a hydrant was still being used up the Escape, I went to the front of the building with the men with a view of making up and removing the Escape, when suddenly I heard Sub-officer Cornford call out "Look out Sir" and saw the building collapsing.

I called out "drop everything and run", but was knocked down by the falling debris and part of the Escape, being subsequently extricated by our men from amongst the debris.

On making enquiry, I found that a message to the effect that the building had collapsed and that several of our men were buried and ambulances were requires had been sent back.

I gave instructions for the debris to be searched for the bodies of our men, then saw the Divisional Officer South who, on hearing of the nature of my injuries ordered me home.

I have since been examined by the District Medical Officer, and placed on the sick list, nature of illness "Injury to Legs". (Signed) ....J.BARROWS

http://www.londonfire.gov.uk/news/LatestNewsRelea ses_LFB150-1918-fire-remains-darkest-day-for- brigade.asp

Coincidentally, the Brigade's former headquarters, built in 1936 and opened a year later, is situated on the Albert Embankment site where the tragic 1918 fire took place.

The names of the seven firefighters, along with others who have lost their lives during service, adorn a memorial inside the building.

21.04.2017

This would be a too sad a note to leave this crawl on, so how about a few more 'origins' before we and set about our final Crawl in this book 'Greenwich and Blackheath (Sailors to Stargazers)'.

Origins

'No Man's Land'

In medieval Britain, towns, and cities has a segregated piece of land outside the city walls (or the town's limits). This land was solely used for execution and torture. Burials were obviously not on the top of their agenda, so bodies were left to decay. This then was considered to be uninhabitable land! At the time the poor who could obtain land potions for free refused to register any title for this land.

Later during the WWI, the land between the trenches also became known as No Man Land, much for the same reason!

'To put one's best foot forward'

Back in Roman times, they believed body was divided down the middle. The right side was considered to be more logical and devoid of irrational thoughts driven by emotions (governed by the head), whereas the left was considered more erratic as it was driven by emotions (governed by the heart).

This later developed into the belief that each individual was followed by two spirits, the good one on the right and the evil one on the left. Tradition then decreed that you always entered a house with the right leg first to allow the good spirit to enter.

This continued throughout history especially amongst sailors who always stepped onto a ship with the right foot first.

Crawl 7
Greenwich and Blackheath (Sailors to Stargazers)

Declaration of personal interest: The Cutty Sark fire has a close spot in my heart as I was the Senior Officer in Charge (London Fire Brigade) of the initial incident, and can still remember how my heart sank coming down the hill to Greenwich from Blackheath, where I could see the flames licking against the breaking dawn sky, and thinking this was part of our heritage going up in flames, to say I had butterflies would be an understatement!

Cutty Sark Ship Ablaze: (21 May 2007)

Speaking to BBC News the Chief Executive of the Cutty Sark Trust, Richard Doughty, said he feared what would be lost in the blaze. "When you lose original fabric, you lose the touch of the craftsman, you lose history itself," he said. "And what is special about the Cutty Sark is the timbers, the iron frames, that went to the South China Seas and to think that that is threatened in any way is unbelievable, it's an unimaginable shock." He said the ship would be "irreplaceable". He added that the Cutty Sark was not just an important part of maritime heritage but an important part of British identity.

Pubs on your route: (Approximately 1.4 miles)

The Mitre – The Coach and Horses – The Gypsy Moth –
The Trafalgar Tavern – The Yacht – The Cutty Sark –
The Plume of feathers

Note: there are no Tube stations really near here (the
nearest being North Greenwich). The nearest mainline
station is at Greenwich, but you also have the option of the
River buses which alight at Greenwich Pier, and the
Dockland Light Railway has two stops near here, one at
Cutty Sark and One at Greenwich (adjacent to mainline
station).

Starting Point

The Mitre

Address: 291 Greenwich High Rd,
London SE10 8NA
Phone: 020 8293 0037
Hours:

Wednesday	9am–11pm
Thursday	9am–11pm
Friday	9am–12am
Saturday	9am–12am
Sunday	9am–10:30pm
Monday	9am–11pm
Tuesday	9am–11pm

The Mitre Hotel was first opened in the 1700s as a coffee shop. It closed down briefly as a result of a fire and re-opened in 1827 as a coaching inn and has been serving the people of Greenwich and its visitors ever since!

It is now recognised by the English Heritage as an important historical site in south-east London.

- Just behind the pub is St Alfege Church – and this has been the site of a church for over a thousand years. Built on the site where St Alfege was beaten to death with animal bones!
- Alfege was born in 954 and gave up his wealth to follow his beliefs; he eventually became Bishop of Winchester but in 1006 he became the 29th Archbishop of Canterbury.
- During this period England and specifically the Kent coast was plagued with looting etc. from pirates from Denmark. In 1011 they laid siege to the City of Canterbury.
- Alfege, given up by one of his own monks, was abducted and transported by ship up the Thames to Greenwich.
- He was initially held and offered up for ransom, but after six months was eventually killed during an Easter celebration by being beaten to death with Ox bones!

Onwards to our next pub,
Route:

On leaving the Mitre turn left towards Greenwich and walk past St Alfeges Church, after the first right (Nelson Road) take the next right under the Arch, Turnpin Lane, and the Coach and Horses is just down there on the left.

Ghost Alert

To the rear of St Alfeges Church is St Alfeges Passage: It is widely assumed that there are many different types of hauntings, from the Malicious (poltergeists), Sexual (succubus), Residual (where a spectre is viewed reliving a past event), Demonic (self-explanatory) and the friendly ghosts who want to interact with the living world (i.e. Casper!) Most ghosts who are either reliving their lives or want to interact with us are normally quite sad (obviously, as if they were happy to be dead they would not be hanging around here!)

The house at 16 St Alfege Passage was a classic Poltergeist. An Edwardian man who had flowing locks, and a mischievous intent. He would if reports are to be believed, wander the house, climbing the stairs and if he felt the need to prove his dominance leave the person seeing the apparition with a feeling of constriction about their throat (choking sensation) then to top it off would provide a show by throwing and moving objects about the place. It is believed that it was a tormented young man who had committed suicide that was responsible for these events, and indeed an 'exorcism' of sorts was carried out by the local priest from St Alfege's church, armed with Holy Water, Bells, Salt, Incense and a bible he set about his task. If he succeeded or not is still not clear, although siting's have not been recorded since!

It's only short walk to our next pub in the Market so let's crack on and then I will point things out when we are there. Over the next three pubs there is little point out en route as they are close together, but don't worry as going around the facts will be coming thick and fast, so make hay while the sun shines.

The Coach and Horses

This pub is located within the Market, which is London's only historic market set within a World Heritage site. This is a lovely place, to sit and drink, and watch the hustle and bustle of the Market.

- The Market's Royal Charter was granted on 19 December 1700 to last for 1,000 years. It was reinforced by an Act of Parliament in 1849.
- Originally housed on the site of the West Gate of the Old Royal Naval College, but in the 1800s it began to expand and overflow into the surrounding area. Filled with lots of little alleyways and passageways, which were dark, it became very difficult to control.
- In an effort to rejuvenate the area and to bring Greenwich's buildings up to a level more in keeping with the Royal Hospital, the market was moved to its current position.

- In 1849 Parliament passed an act that enabled the Hospital to collect rent from the traders, this was in addition to the powers of the original charter.
- This act allowed for trading to be undertaken two days a week, but 1905 a newly added bylaw allowed six days a week trading except for Sundays, Christmas and Bank Holidays.
- The market gradually declined throughout the 1900s until in the 1980s it saw its revival.

Route: Walk north through the market and exit onto College approach. Turn left and the Spanish Galleon is just down on your left.

Again a short walk until the next watering hole and the only thing of note en-route is the entrance Gate to the Royal Naval College which is on your right as you exit the market, but we will cover that more in detail as we go around.

The Spanish Galleon

Address: 48 Greenwich Church St,
London SE10 9BL
Phone: 020 8858 3664
Hours:

Sunday	11am–11pm
Monday	11am–11pm
Tuesday	11am–11pm
Wednesday	11am–11pm
Thursday	11am–11pm
Friday	11am–11pm
Saturday	11am–11pm

- This pub was designed and built in 1834 by Joseph Kay during the reign of William IV – The Sailor King.
- When being updated in 1985, a 19th Century sailors' uniform was discovered in a bricked-up

room in the cellar. This is now on display in the pub.

- Named after paintings in the Royal Naval College which depicted sea battles against the Spanish Armada.

Ghost Alert

It is believed that the pub is haunted by a black dog (hellhound) named Shuk, which manifests itself when things get a little boisterous, a local folklore was meeting in the pub and they did their best to summon it but to avail. There are numerous Hell Hound phantoms across London but it does appear that their bark is worse than their bite, as their image is enough to scare people on its own!

Route:

Come out of the Spanish galleon and head north towards the River Thames down Greenwich Church Street which right in front of you. Just down on your right is our next watering hole, The Gipsy Moth, it is from here the history starts coming through.

The Gipsy Moth

Address: 60 Greenwich Church St,
London SE10 9BL
Phone: 020 8858 0786
Hours:

Saturday	11am–12am
Sunday	11am–11pm
Monday	11am–11pm
Tuesday	11am–11pm
Wednesday	11am–11pm
Thursday	11am–11pm
Friday	11am–12am

- Originally built in 1795, and called the Wheatsheaf changed its name from to Gipsy Moth in 1975 (no conspiracy over the numbers).
- This was to mark the arrival in Greenwich of Gypsy Moth IV. This was the boat in which Francis Chichester completed the first single handed around the world voyage in 1967. It was

nestled in the dry dock next to the Cutty Sark, but in 2016 set sail again for a tour of Britain.

- Francis Chichester was knighted by Queen Elizabeth II on the steps in front of the Royal Naval College. The Queen used the same sword that was used to knight Sir Frances Drake, in 1581, on board his ship the Golden Hind at Deptford in the presence of Queen Elizabeth I.

As stated earlier, the information gets quite intense now, so it may be worth having a drink while reading this lot before moving off.

Just outside the Pub in front of the Thames, stands the Cutty Sark in dry dock.

The Cutty Sark Ship (The pub comes later!):
- Launched on the 22nd November 1869 the Cutty Sark was a composite Tea Clipper Ship (made of wood and metal), having a gross tonnage of 963 tonnes, and 11 miles of rigging around 3 masts and 32 sails.

- The Cutty Sark was used predominantly to transport tea from China to England although it did ship Wool from Australia later in its life.
- It is widely believed that steamships brought the tea clipper era to an end. However, it appears to have been a combination of steam ships and the opening of the Suez Canal
- Tea Clippers would have to go around the Horn of Africa, whereas steamships could take the much quicker Suez Canal route.
- In 1957 after falling into disrepair she was restored and put in dry dock at Greenwich.
- 21 May 2007, an industrial vacuum cleaner which had been left on was deemed to be the cause of the fire starting in the early hours of that Monday morning.
- I was the initial Incident Commander of the eight pump fire and remember vividly the sinking feeling in the pit of my stomach as I drove down from Blackheath and saw the flames rising out of the darkened sky below.
- I won't bore you with all the details, but just to say the Fire Crews that day were amazing, and it's through their actions the fire did not destroy the whole ship.
- If you are interested, look up on the internet the details of the fire and see how many people claim to have been in charge of the incident…and note their names! I will leave it there.

Ghost Alert

- The Cutty Sark and its figurehead 'nannie' are also associated with the 'dark arts' as their names are linked to a Robert Burns poem Tam O'Shanter (1791).

- The tale is told that a man named Tam O'Shanter, whilst riding home late one night, his route took him past a churchyard where he saw a coven of witches dancing around a bonfire.
- Most were stereotypically old and ugly, but one was 'hot'. Her name was Nannie, and she wore nothing but a nightie (a sark) that had been 'cut' short, and displayed her legs.
- Tam was more than happy to see her in this attire, he exclaimed loudly, "Weel done, cutty sark!"
- At this the witches, who were just a little bit peeved, gave chase.
- Nannie, being the youngest, was soon leading the chasing pack, but Tam realising that if he could get across the bridge he would be safe, (legend has it witches cannot cross water!) he drove his horse onwards for the bridge.
- But Nannie was quick and was just able the grasp the horse's tail, but this was not enough to stop the pair as they were riding so fast, but she did manage to pull the tail right off and was left clasping it in her hand as they crossed the bridge.
- Nannie grasping the horse's tail is forever enshrined as the figurehead of the Cutty Sark, and can still be seen in the exhibition under the Cutty Sark.
- So apart from nannie, an unknown spirit has also been seen keeping his watch from the top of the crow's nest

Just across from the Cutty Sark is the:

Greenwich Foot Tunnel

History: Built at the turn of the 20th century this tunnel crosses beneath the River Thames and links Greenwich to the Isle of Dogs. This gave free access to the north of the river for people who worked in the docks.

Ghosts Alert:

If you have time and you feel brave enough, especially at night, stroll through the 370 metres and see if you experience the distant echoes which are heard, along with the deep sense of foreboding and being followed, or maybe not! *(But this is not on our route, so if you cross you must come back to continue!)*

Route: As you face the Thames head right down alongside the river until you come to the next pub, The Trafalgar Tavern.

On your route, some things to look out for:

Ghost Alert
The SS Great Eastern

- As you follow our route along the Thames, just a little way from the Cutty Sark you may be lucky (if the time is right) and see the image of a Ghost Ship! This is reputed to be the spectre of Isambard Kingdom Brunel's last ship: The Great Eastern.
- The ship was alleged to be cursed before it was even launched. Rumours of workers dying, even children (who were sometimes used as labour back then) being trapped between the hull skins, did not help with its reputation.

309

- Then it goes and fails to launch! Definitely cursed!
- Then people heard hammering from inside the hull skins below deck (maybe it was the trapped children trying to get out!)
- The SS Great Eastern was a massive 22,500-ton steamship, it was so big exiting docks could not cope with its size.
- Her near 700-foot length, and weight would remain as the largest ship of its kind for another 40 years.
- This was the largest ship in the World at the time.
- On the 3rd November 1857, the ship then christened Leviathan failed on the initial launch. Brunel had decided to launch her sideways but she only slipped down a few feet, and then stopped.
- 3 months later on 31st January 1858 she was finally launched as the SS Great Eastern.
- The remains of the slipway can be seen today. If you look to the Thames it's on the other side of the river to your left. Should you wish to visit the site the address is: Napier Ave, Isle of Dogs, London E14 3TD (you could walk there via the Greenwich Foot tunnel!)

On your right-hand side: The Royal Naval College Grounds, and nowadays Greenwich University Campus. Previously, on this site stood the Royal Naval hospital and The Palace of Placentia.

- There has been a royal manor house in Greenwich since the reign of Edward I, better known as Longshanks (1272 to 1307),
- After inheriting the manor of Greenwich in 1417, Humphrey, Duke of Gloucester had a palace built

there on the banks of the Thames, known as *Bella Court (completed in 1428 later to become the Palace of Placentia)*.

- Humphrey was quite unique in the royal bloodline, he was known as the 'son, brother and uncle of kings!' This was because; wait for it, Son of King Henry IV, Brother of Henry V and the Uncle of Henry VI!

- The estate surrounding Bella Court, some 200 acres, which had been owned by the Abbey of St Peter at Ghent, reverted back to the Crown in 1427, and was then given by Henry VI to his uncle Humphrey, Duke of Gloucester, who enclosed the park in 1433.

- Later James I, built a 12-foot-high brick wall around the whole park, much of which remains today.

- Following this a little while later he was again given further grants to completely redesign Bella Court and to build a castle on current site of the Royal Observatory (then called Greenwich Castle).

- Constructed in 1433 it was thought to originally comprise a moated tower. It was enlarged in 1525 to include a second tower.

- It was a very lovely place with handsome grounds and a river frontage. So nice in fact that Margeurite of Anjou, the rather pushy wife of Henry VI, devised a way for the place to be hers.

- She dreamt up a fantastic scary story (as it would have been back then!) and accused the Dukes wife of acting like a witch, and creating what we know now as a 'voodoo' doll in the likeness of the her husband Edward VI and sticking it with pins!

- The King obviously appalled arrested Humphrey and he died in custody.
- Low and behold the property was sequestered back to Crown and Margeurite got her way!
- It was not as popular as Eltham Palace at first, but it location meant it was used regularly, and was convenient for the docks at Woolwich (Henry VIII's flagship The Great Harry was built here) and Deptford.
- In 1485 King Henry VII ascended to the throne of England and straight away made a 'bee line' for the Palace of Placentia and invested heavily in its structure. He enlarged the palace, as well as finishing off the Tower of Greenwich Castle.
- Wanting to be seen to have spent wisely, King Henry VII spent a great deal of his time at Greenwich and it was here his wife, Elizabeth of York, gave birth to Good Old King Henry VIII.
- Henry VIII made the Palace of Placentia his primary residence, and enjoyed socialising by throwing vast banquets and setting aside land in the park to host jousting competitions.
- The first masquerade ball ever seen in England, was hosted by Henry and his then wife Catherine as part of their Christmas celebrations in1516. As was written at the time:

"The King this year kept the feast of Christmas at Greenwich, where was such an abundance of the viands served to all corners of any honest behaviour as hath been few times seen."

- During the years that followed, The Palace of Placentia heard the patter of tiny feet throughout the Royal Residence as Mary I and Elizabeth I were both born here.
- The grounds, within the Palace of Placentia are where Sir Walter Raleigh was reputed to have thrown his cloak down over a puddle, in order that Queen Elizabeth would not get her feet wet.
- Shakespeare had an association with Greenwich as he performed two comedies in front of Elizabeth I at Greenwich Palace.
- During the first half of the 17th century both King James I and King Charles I kept the Palace of Placentia as their principle residence.
- However, following the Civil War things changed. Once Oliver Cromwell had taken control, he tried to sell off a lot of crown property, but the Palace at Greenwich attracted no buyers.
- Not being able to glean any funds from the Palace he turned it into a biscuit factory! (Also for a time it was a used as prisoner of war camp.)
- When Charles II ascended to the throne the once beautiful Palace was now a sad run-down building which he decreed should be demolished and be replaced with a new resplendent Palace of Freestone.
- In 1695 the Greenwich Castle was demolished when the Royal Observatory was constructed.

- For whatever reason only part of the new Palace was ever completed, as the favoured places of residence had moved from Greenwich to Kensington and Hampton Court.
- The building which remained was converted and merged with the New Naval hospital which was established in 1692 on the site. This is now part of Greenwich University.
- The centrepiece of the hospital was the dining hall and in 1708 James Thornhill was appointed to decorate its walls and ceiling with suitably maritime imagery.
- This appointment was early in his career, and being very keen to land the commission he did not negotiate a price for his work, just asking they pay him a reasonable fee! They would not take advantage of that then!
- So for a job which nearly took him 20 years he was paid £7000 based on a rate of £1 per square yard for the walls and £3 per square yard for the ceilings.
- Fortunately, the magnificence of his achievement gained due recognition and Thornhill was eventually knighted.
- If you look at the bottom right of the mural on the wall, Thornhill painted a self-portrait with his hand out, as if asking for more money!
- Today the only part of the old Palace of Placentia that remains is the 17th century Queen's House, which was commissioned by King James I.
- In 1806, three months after the Battle of Trafalgar the previous October, the body of Horatio Nelson was brought to lie in state in the Painted Hall. A plaque marks the spot where his

coffin was placed before it was taken for burial in the crypt of St Paul's Cathedral.

- Greenwich is also loved by Hollywood and the Film industry, lots of blockbusters have been shot here, Les Miserables, Thor, Tomb Raider to name but a few.

The Trafalgar Tavern

Address: Park Row, London SE10 9NW
Phone: 020 8858 2909
Hours:

Wednesday	12–11pm
Thursday	12–11pm
Friday	12pm–12am
Saturday	10am–12am
Sunday	12–11pm
Monday	12–11pm
Tuesday	12–11pm

- There has been a pub on this site since the 11th century with the current building being in situ since 1837.
- In1837 it was named in as homage to Admiral Nelson whose body lay in state at the Painted

Hall in nearby Greenwich Hospital, following his return from the Victory and Trafalgar.

- It is even mentioned in Charles Dickens Little Dorritt.
- Many famous people, including Dickens and Thackeray, have been associated with this hostelry, especially in Victorian days.
- Even parliamentarians got in on the riverside gem, travelling from Westminster to enjoy the house specialty a whitebait supper, still available today.
- In 1915, the Tavern closed, due to World War I and became a home for aged seamen. Between the WWI and WWII it became a working man's club.
- It reverted back to a pub in 1965, and has since become a symbol of Greenwich.

Ghost Alert

A regular apparition dressed in Victorian or Georgian clothing haunts the main bar. He is seen sitting at the bar or the piano drinking beer. He then and walks through the wall where the fireplace is! In the olden time this is the site where the door was, and as everyone knows ghosts remain in their time.

This appears to be a friendly spirit as previous owners have apparently spoken to him!

In the cellar though, beer crates have been seen to be moving across the floor!

Route:
Walk alongside the pub about 50 yards down Crane Street until you reach our next stop off, The Yacht.

The Yacht

Address: 5-7 Crane St, London SE10 9NP
Phone: 020 8858 0175
Hours:

Wednesday	12–11pm
Thursday	12–11pm
Friday	12–11pm
Saturday	12–10:30pm
Sunday	12–10:30pm
Monday	12–11pm
Tuesday	12–11pm

The Yacht known locally as the First Pub in the West, as it is as close as you can get to the West of the Meridian line in Greenwich! The pub was modelled on one of the lounge bars in the liner the Queen Mary and has historical pictures adorning the walls and a very traditional feel about the place.

Not a lot if history here compared with other pubs but a nice place to eat and drink.

Route: Come out of pub and turn left again, carry on down this road which leads into Ballast Quay where you will find our next watering hole. The Cutty Sark.

On your route you will pass on your right:

Trinity Hospital

The hospital was founded as alms houses by Henry Howard, Earl of Northampton. A board near its entrance reads: "Since 1617 it has provided a home for 21 retired gentlemen of Greenwich." The hospital was rebuilt in 1812 in its present Gothic style, and is still in use. The charity is run by Mercer.

One feature is common to all alms-houses is that the chapel is always sited prominently, this was done to remind the aged residents that their thoughts should be turning looking forward to next life!

Trinity did not however open its doors to all and sundry. When it opened in 1617 it had certain pre-requisites before allowing you to reside there. "No common beggar, drunkard, whore-hunter, haunter of taverns nor ale houses, nor unclean person infected with any foul disease, nor any that is blind, or so impotent as he is not able, at the time of his admission, to come to prayers daily..."

https://books.google.co.uk/books?id=vqJfAAAAcAAJ

Rules nowadays are more relaxed, but previously it was not so. Here is a typical daily timetable:

6am: (8am in winter) rise, dress, and say prayers

9am: Service in chapel (or St Alfege Church on Wednesday and Friday)

11am: Free time (gardening and housework)

3pm: Church or chapel service followed by free time ('weekly correction on Saturday')

6pm: Supper in the hall

9pm: Bedtime

http://carolineld.blogspot.co.uk/2008/09/almshouses-in-south-east-london-open.html

The Cutty Sark Pub

Address: 5-7 Crane St, London SE10 9NP
Phone: 020 8858 0175
Hours:

Wednesday	12–11pm
Thursday	12–11pm
Friday	12–11pm
Saturday	12–10:30pm
Sunday	12–10:30pm
Monday	12–11pm
Tuesday	12–11pm

Records are not fully available for how long a tavern has been on this site, but it's known that there was one here before 1805, (when the pub we see today was established) which was The Green Man (1792 maps show the existence of The Green Man).

In 1810, it was known as the Union Tavern, and changed its name to the Cutty Sark when it first came to Greenwich in 1951, and found its permanent home in the dry dock in 1954.

Its low beams, wooden floors etc. all give the feeling of being inside an 18th century sailing ship.

Route: A bit of a trek now to our last pub. Turn left out of the pub and follow the road which is Lassell Street. At the junction with Trafalgar Road turn right and then first left into Maze Hill. Going up Maze Hill take the first right into Park Vista the Plume of Feathers is just down here on your right.

On your route there is not much of note to draw your attention to; however that will change when we reach the next pub.

The Plume of Feathers

Address: 19 Park Vista, London SE10 9LZ
Phone: 020 8858 1661
Hours:

Wednesday 12–11pm

Thursday 12–11pm

Friday 11am–12am

Saturday 11am–12am

Sunday 12–11pm

Monday 12–11pm

Tuesday 12–11pm

- The Plume of Feathers, a quaint old English pub just outside Greenwich Park, dates back to 1691 and, given its position, has a plethora of naval and maritime artefacts.
- First called The Prince of Wales, and later changed to the Plume of feathers in 1726.

- It's also bang on the Meridian Line and you can work out pub opening times in the rest of the world as you sup your pints.
- William III and Mary II were on throne when the pub first opened for business.
- The road outside Plume of Feathers was once the main road passing through Greenwich to Woolwich, until a newer road was built about 100 yards north by Lord Romney, and called Romeny Road which is still used today (A206).
- It divided the park from the Tudor Palace, which stood by the river. Along the road stood Tudor buildings connected with the Palace. It is said that it was in one of these building that Edward VI, Henry VIII's son, died at the young age of 16, having been ill for many years.
- The Plume of Feathers is, of course, the heraldic badge of the Prince of Wales. Although the use of three ostrich feathers can be traced back to Edward, the Black Prince
- In 1884 Greenwich's meridian was adopted by the world as the prime meridian of the world, so from day The Plume of Feathers became the first pub in the Eastern half of the world, a claim which still stand today!
- So outside the pub turn right and follow Park Vista to the end where you can see the entrance to the Greenwich Maritime Museum, and on the left of that Greenwich Park. Although our crawl ended in the Plume of Feathers it would be remiss of me not to talk about The Queens House/Greenwich Park & Royal Observatory.
- Let's start with the Queens House, we spoke earlier about the Royal Naval hospital etc., so as

we are faced with the buildings in front of us here we go:

Queens House

This is the First Classical building in England. Designed by Inigo Jones.

1. Commissioned by Anne of Denmark (King James I's wife). Given to her, according to some rumours, by the King as an apology for swearing at her! Although she never got see her Palace as she died in 1619.
2. It wasn't until Henrietta Maria (King Charles I's wife) took control, that is was completed in 1638.
3. A major change came following the outbreak of the Civil War, Henrietta was forced to flee for her life in 1643, unfortunately her husband was not so lucky and in 1643 he was beheaded for treason on January 30, 1649, as England became a commonwealth.
4. **The Palladian style of the Queen's House in Greenwich was the influence for the design of the United States White House.**

Ghost Alert:

The year is 1966 when a couple of retired Canadian tourists visit the Queens House and as you do, took a series of holiday snaps, it was only when they had them developed did the spectre manifest itself. This has never been explained!

- The whole of the World Heritage Centre area is shrouded in mystery and awe and owes its existence to an accusation of witchcraft. Remember the Duke of Gloucester's wife earlier!
- As we discovered Henry VIII loved this place, and it is believed the place is haunted by the ghost of a red-headed woman with a low-cut corset.

Investigators believe this could be the spirit of none other than Elizabeth the First (Henry's daughter), who was said to walk 'in a shower of bejewelled pins' when she disembarked at the Greenwich docks.

- They say that her spirit walks the corridors of the old palace, taking her out into the docks around the Cutty Sark. Maybe she is off meeting Nannie.
- Another famous spectral figure which has been seen is reputedly to be Anne Boleyn, but this is assumed, as they are wearing Elizabethan clothing it could also be one of Liz's handmaidens!

Greenwich Park & Observatory

- Greenwich Park, was fully enclosed in 1433, and is Britain's oldest such park. When Henry V's bother inherited it in 1427 it became Royal property and remains so today.
- Greenwich Park was home to Greenwich Castle, which served as one of King Henry VIII's many hunting lodges.
- Visitors today can still see the fallen tree where Queen Bess took refreshments in her youth. A plaque is in place which tells the story, see below:
- The Royal Observatory was commissioned by King Charles II and its location site chosen by Sir Christopher Wren in 1675.
- The Longitude Act of 1714, gave the Observatory another role, that of the home of the Prime Meridian, an essential navigational tool for sailors.

- Sir Christopher Wren well known for his architectural masterpieces was also once a Professor of Astronomy (Oxford University), which made him a prime candidate for King Charles II when he set about looking for someone to build an observatory. He was also credited with choosing the site in Greenwich.

- Hard for us to comprehend, but the original cost of building the Royal Observatory was £520, which was way over budget by the amount of £20! Mind you this was back in 1675!

- The world's first weather forecast was issued from Greenwich Royal Observatory in 1848 by James Glaisher

- In 1884 US president Chester Arthur called for an International Meridian Conference in Washington, here a vote was held to determine which city would be the Prime Meridian. Greenwich won! So on the 13th October 1884, history was made as Greenwich was declared the Prime Meridian for the world.

- In the 19th Century, sailors from all over the world relied on Greenwich when setting their own chronometers and helped Greenwich Mean Time to become the universal standard.

- Finished in 1893, the 28-inch Refracting Telescope in the Royal Observatory is the largest of its kind in the UK and the seventh largest in the world.

- The Shepherd Gate Clock is one of the earliest examples of an electric synchronised (or slave) clock.

- The Time Ball atop of the observatory is one of the earliest time signals. The first was installed in

Portsmouth in 1829, whilst the Greenwich Time ball was installed in 1833.

- It works such, that at 1255, it raises up its mast to drop exactly at 1300, allowing ships' captains to accurately set their chronometers before they set sail.
- It can be easily seen from the River through the purpose built gaps in the Buildings.
- The Public Standards of Length can be found here and represent the exact lengths under the imperial measurement system. The brass pegs for each measurement are spaced far enough apart that a rod of exact length (be it a yard, two feet, one foot, etc.) should fit snuggly between them.

So that's your lot!

All that is now needed is to somehow put an ending to this series of Crawls!

Hopefully you are still sober, and your liver is okay!

I am not sure if you did all of the crawls in order or chose just to do one at a time, or maybe just one specific one for the area you know. It was my intention that you picked up some nice titbits of information to bore people with at parties, but most of all I hope you enjoyed the journey.

London is a great city with a wealth of hidden treasures which people walk past on a daily basis. This is a wonder to me, for a city which has millions of people, who commute, work and live here, there are so many which are myopic that they fail to see what's around them.

This fact was brought home to me when I visited another great City (although not as good a London!) Paris. I visited the Louvre, and of course I went to see the Mona Lisa. I was a bit taken aback about how small it was, but it was okay! Hey, I am no art expert.

However, whilst the massed crowd all jockeyed for position to glimpse her enigmatic smile (see I can appreciate art!), their eyes were fixed on the painting by Leonardo Da Vinci, trying to snap a photo or 'selfie!' they had no eyes for anything else. As is my way, I was looking all around, but when I was there hardly anyone else turned away from 'Mona' and therefore missed the 'bigger picture'. On the wall opposite is the Louvre's largest painting, The Wedding at Cana, by Paolo Veronese which is fantastic, but hardly anyone sees it.

The same can be said of London; people rush from place to place, catching buses, taxis, trains and tubes, reading their papers, or phones/tablets and in all their daily trials, they miss the beauty of London. A city with over 2000 years of history should not be ignored or taken for granted. Sometimes, tourists know more about London than its citizens do!

So hopefully these crawls have allowed you to have the time to get a glimpse of our great city from a different perspective.

Lord Byron tried to sum up London:

> *A MIGHTY mass of brick, and smoke,*
> *and shipping,*
> *Dirty and dusky, but as wide as eye*
> *Could reach, with here and there a sail*
> *just skipping*
> *In sight, then lost amidst the forestry*
> *Of masts; a wilderness of steeples*   5
> *peeping*
> *On tiptoe through their sea-coal*
> *canopy;*
> *A huge, dun cupola, like a foolscap*
> *crown*
> *On a fool's head, and there is London*
> *Town*

But even this overall tongue in cheek description fails (in my opinion) to capture London and all of its glories. From the darkened alleys where Jack the Ripper stalked and killed his victims, to the splendour of the Palaces of Kings; from the History of 2000 years to the Folklore tales of old; from the Water to the Land and from the Brewery to the Pub. London is a city which has something for everyone. Samuel Johnson was quite succinct when he said

"Why, Sir, you find no man, at all intellectual, who is willing to leave London. No, Sir, when a man is tired of London, he is tired of life; for there is in London all that life can afford."

So, if you stumbled through all seven crawls and are still standing you deserve a medal. If you managed to you did the Monopoly Pub crawl as well you deserve a citation on the medal, but as I do not have any, pat yourselves on the back. Well Done!

To prove that it's not all about drinking see if you can add some responses to the statement below.

Have you learned anything?

The basics!

- How to handle your drink?
- That you need to wear comfortable shoes?
- An umbrella is always handy in London?
- Unexpected learning!
- London has a wealth of hidden histories/stories that people are unaware of.
- Ghosts are seen throughout London, and are still fascinating.
- Far from being safe from fire London seems to have been forged from the flames of disasters. Hopefully we have learnt from our ancestors!

- Theatres when first built had no idea about fire safety
- London's history can be directly traced through it pubs.
- And London is a truly great city and different from anywhere else.
- A simple look at London through Beer Goggles has hopefully stoked your enthusiasm to find out more.

Well Done

Sources and Further Reading

In writing this book, I have tried to verify what I believed I already knew from living my whole life in London. Throughout my life I have fed my appetite for the unusual by taking part in various walks around London (some information provided on some of these walks I have to say does possess a little 'poetic license' at times for the 'tourist') reading various books, and researching quizzes I have written in the past.

London, I find is a fascinating City, and holds more folklore, legend, history and facts than most cities I have visited, and you could spend a lifetime reading and not discover everything. During this project I have used the following books and websites trying to substantiate the factoids contained there. If I have whetted your appetite please read on.

Books:

LEYLAND SIMON. 2014. *A Curious Guide to London*. Great Britain: Transworld Publishers
ROUD STEVE. 2008. *London Lore. The Legends and Traditions of the World's most vibrant City.* London: Arrow Books
HALIDAY STEPHEN. 2011. *Amazing & Extraordinary Facts London.* London: A David & Charles Book

Websites:
http://www.spookyisles.com/2012/07/the-bones-of-st-brides-church/
https://www.ianvisits.co.uk/london-alleys/

http://www.historic-uk.com/HistoryMagazine/DestinationsUK/Newgate-Prison-Wall/

http://www.walksoflondon.co.uk/35/true-ghost-stories-the-co.shtml

http://www.london-ghost-tour.com/ghosts-of-the-west-end.htm

http://www.roh.org.uk/about/history

http://www.telegraph.co.uk/travel/destinations/europe/united-kingdom/england/london/articles/London-Underground-150-fascinating-Tube-facts/

http://londonist.com/2011/07/london-facts-that-arent-actually-true

http://www.shadyoldlady.com/location.php?loc=925

https://www.google.com/maps/d/viewer?mid=1g06yOJHD6OORLaAM2IMKHeMtUDc&hl=en_US&ll=51.512889089653505%2C-0.12930900000003476&z=16

www.historic-uk.com

www.eastlondonhistory.co.uk

www.historytoday.com

www.secret-london.co.uk

www.capitalpunishmentuk.org

http://londonist.com/2012/01/in-search-of-londons-execution-sites

http://www.historytoday.com/richard-cavendish/execution-captain-kidd#sthash.SNl0cHgR.dpuf

http://www.thamespolicemuseum.org.uk/h_wappingcoalriots_1.html

http://www.townoframsgate.co.uk/history.html

http://www.skdocks.co.uk/the-docks/our-heritage

http://www.britannia.com/hiddenlondon/ireland_yard.html

http://www.capitalpunishmentuk.org/behead.html

http://londonist.com/2012/01/in-search-of-londons-execution-sites

http://www.haunted-london.com/haunted-london-pubs.html

https://www.spookythings.iofw.co.uk/?page_id=200

http://www.paulkavanagh.com/en/Weird-Strange-London-Facts.html

http://archive.museumoflondon.org.uk

http://www.uncoveringlondon.co.uk/st-george-the-martyr-clock.html

http://www.timetravel-britain.com/articles/london/pubs.shtml

http://www.localhistories.org/southwark.html

http://www.wegoplaces.me/haunted-places-in-london/

http://www.ghostclub.org.uk/viaduct.htm

http://www.telegraph.co.uk

https://funlondontours.com

http://www.whatsonstage.com/london-theatre/news/20-amazing-theatre-facts_34626.html

http://www.arthurlloyd.co.uk/HerMajestysTheatre.htm

http://www.real-british-ghosts.com/haunted-theaters.html

http://www.mayfaireccentrics.com/

http://londondetour.blogspot.co.uk/2013/02/greenwich-park-secrets-shhhh.html

http://www.shakespeare-online.com/theatre/theroyalpalaces.html

http://www.thegreenwichphantom.co.uk/2007/05/underground-greenwich-3-jack-cades-cavern/

https://www.buzzfeed.com/patricksmith/54-amazing-facts-about-london-that-will-blow-your-mind?utm_term=.otjLE4zdm#.qmJn3JlLo

http://www.historic-uk.com/HistoryMagazine/DestinationsUK/Burlington-Arcade-the-Burlington-Beadles/

http://www.greenwichworldheritage.org/

http://www.british-history.ac.uk/old-new-london/vol4/pp345-359